How To

Activate Miracles In Your Life and Ministry

How To
Activate Miracles In Your Life and Ministry

by

Burnie Davis

HARRISON HOUSE
Tulsa, Oklahoma

Unless otherwise indicated,
all Scripture quotations are taken from
the *King James Version* of the Bible.

New Testament quotations marked NIV are from
the *New International Version*.

How To Activate Miracles In Your Life and Ministry
ISBN 0-89274-230-5

Burnie Davis Global Ministries
Box 7148
Pasadena, Texas 77505

Published by Harrison House, Inc.
P. O. Box 35035
Tulsa, Oklahoma 74135

Printed in the United States of America.

Acknowledgments

I am very grateful to Dr. Joel French and his wife Jane for all the help they gave me in arranging this book.

Contents

Foreword

I am very pleased to be able to introduce you to Burnie Davis' exciting book on miracles. This book has been needed for a long time, and I am so glad that God instructed Burnie to release this knowledge for the Body of Christ.

I have said to many people over the years that Burnie is a man who knows how to have miracles. Many ministries have miracles, but very few of them know why or how! That used to bother me. If a person doesn't know why or how he does something, then he can't teach others to do it. But Burnie Davis knows how to have a miracle ministry and he knows why he has one.

I have known Burnie and Dolly and their family for many years and have watched them be used of God to help many people.

I have been present to see many of the miracles Burnie talks about in this book. They are real; I saw them.

I feel like I have taken courses for missionary evangelism taught by Burnie because I have observed the successful missionary and learned so much from him.

My wife Jackie and I were *new* missionaries when we met Burnie. He told me then that all I needed was "some miracles under my belt." He gave me some opportunities to preach and some people to pray for, and God began to confirm His Word with signs following.

If you will read this book and combine its instructions with God's Word, you too will be used of God to meet the needs of people. You will become a "people helper," giving Living Bread to dying men around the world.

For the only Cause that counts,

Terry L. Mize

Preface

I have seen countless numbers of outstanding miracles in my ministry both in the United States and in many foreign countries. I have also seen the dead brought back to life on several occasions. You will read about many of these miracles in this book. In fact, miracles have become a way of life for my whole family.

I praise God for all the miracles in my ministry. I am also thankful that I have been able to teach many others how to activate the working of miracles in their own ministries. We teach others partly by showing them how I learned to move into a miracle ministry. That is the reason so much of my own personal testimony is presented in this book.

I have often been asked how I came into a ministry of miracles. Really there is not much that *I* have done; rather, it is a gift from God. God has given me the gift of supernatural faith and of the working of miracles. However, I know that *every* believer can have miracles in his own ministry.

It is my prayer that every person, who reads this book and sincerely desires miracles in his ministry, will come to realize that God desires for every believer to minister the Word with signs following.

In Mark 16:17 Jesus said, *And these signs shall follow them that believe; In my name shall they . . .* (perform miracles).

If you are a believer, then signs should and can follow your ministry. How shall the miracles come? **In the name of Jesus.** In His name we shall set the captives free, cast out devils, and perform miracles of healing.

In the book of Acts, we see that the early Church understood this fact and moved into the ministry of miracles without hesitation. Acts 6:8 says, *Stephen, full of faith and power, did great wonders and miracles among the people.*

The ministry of miracles is world shaking. Miracles are needed to shake the world. Miracles are the true witness of the power of God to the unbeliever.

In Acts 4:31 we read, *When they had prayed, the place was shaken where they were assembled together.* These preachers moved with the earth-shaking power of the Holy Ghost.

And as shown in Acts 5:12-14, their preaching was witnessed with evidence: *And by the hands of the apostles were many signs and wonders wrought among the people . . . And believers were the more added to the Lord, multitudes both of men and women.*

There is only one scriptural way to reach the millions of people living on the earth today who have not heard the gospel message of Jesus Christ. And that way is **by demonstrating the mighty power** of the risen Christ of God by performing mighty miracles before their eyes through the name of Jesus. In the book of Acts multitudes were won to Christ when they witnessed the miracles performed by the apostles.

In this book, you will travel with me through my past and see how I was able to move from a timid adolescence into a dynamic ministry, identified with many outstanding miracles for Jesus Christ.

I pray that, as you read, the Father of our Lord Jesus Christ will open the eyes of your understanding and grant you the spirit of revelation knowledge. Allow God's Spirit to speak to you through this book. I set my faith in agreement with you that you will move into faith for the working of miracles in your own life and ministry.

— Burnie Davis

1
Heavenly Visions

The year I turned twelve was a year of great spiritual experiences for me. I was born, the oldest of three sons, into a Full Gospel preacher's home. My two younger brothers, Gerald and Rick, are also Full Gospel preachers. Mom and Dad always taught us boys the Word of God. In fact, when we put our shoes on each morning, Dad was beside our beds reading the Bible and drilling the Word of God into us.

Dad was pastoring an Assembly of God church in Orange, Texas, and Rev. Gladys Pearson was conducting a revival there when I received the baptism of the Holy Spirit.

Reflecting on that glorious night so long ago now, it seems I can remember every detail, so vividly was it fixed in my mind. Rev. Pearson was a well-known evangelist and preached under a heavy anointing. A great number were saved and filled with the Holy Spirit every night.

I had sat in the services for several nights and the Holy Spirit just suddenly seemed to reach out and grab my heart. I remember it was raining that night. But it seemed always to be raining in Orange, a small city on the Gulf Coast.

I went to the altar after the service, knelt, and began to cry. I don't know why — I just cried. I couldn't stop myself. Then several people knelt beside me and began praying. After a while it seemed as if buckets of liquid love were being poured over me. I felt light as a feather, as if I didn't weigh a pound.

And a strange language began coming into my mind. At first, I could only whisper the strange words. But then, with the encouragement of those around me, I began singing praises to God in the strange new language. When I came to myself, I was lying on my back in front of the altar. I would lie quietly for a few minutes, and then continue praising God in my new language.

How long I lay there on the floor, I don't remember. I was not even aware of the people around me, so lost in the Spirit was I. It was during one of those quiet periods that I was carried away in the Spirit.

In the vision I saw myself as a grown man, standing on a very crude and rough-looking platform, surrounded by a sea of dark-skinned people. As far as I could see in the vision, there were foreigners. I was the only white person.

Then, in the vision, I took up a microphone and began preaching to the people. I told them that Jesus Christ would save their souls and heal their sick bodies. How long I preached, I don't know. They told me later that while I lay on the floor I was really speaking under a heavy anointing in my heavenly language. I spoke for nearly a half hour as if I were really preaching, with hand movements and facial expressions.

In the vision, I saw myself give the altar call, and thousands of people crowded toward the crude platform for salvation. I then prayed for the sick *en masse*, as I do now; and all through the great crowd, I saw people being healed of various ailments and conditions. Cripples threw down crutches and walked. Blind eyes were opened.

Up to that time Dad had never held any crusades, having served as pastor in several churches. I had never been to a crusade even in the States, let alone in a foreign country. This tremendous spiritual experience and the vivid vision left me in a daze. It seemed that the power of God stayed with me for several days afterwards. Rather than playing with other kids, I kept to myself during the day, meditating on what I had seen in the vision. Sometimes after going to bed at night, I would lay awake for hours praying in tongues.

It was several years later that Dad first began conducting miracle crusades in churches and tents. I seemed to inherit the gift and spirit of miracles through his ministry when I was a boy.

I remember one particular tent crusade Dad held in Douglas, Arizona, when I was about eighteen or nineteen years old. A prominent doctor carried his small son to the healing line. The boy had been born without bones in his legs. You could have wrung his legs like a dish rag, they were so limp.

Dad took the boy from his father's arms and prayed for him. Then Dad did something that shocked that huge audience and almost gave the good doctor a heart attack. (And I'll admit to nearly fainting myself!) Dad held that small boy out at arms' length and dropped him to the floor. There was a loud gasp in the audience. But somewhere between Dad's arms and the floor, God created new bones in the boy's legs, because he landed squarely on his feet and walked away. True, he walked unsteadily and needed help — but he walked, something he had never done before in his life!

God performed a creative miracle in that boy's boneless legs. I witnessed the miracle with my own eyes.

From the time I was thirteen or so, I witnessed many such miracles in Dad's ministry. Miracles became almost commonplace, something to be expected in every service.

But Mom and Dad continued to drill the Word of God into us boys. We were taught that the Word was the important thing. The great feelings, the emotional high, and the miraculous healings were wonderful, we were taught, but all were a result of God's confirming His Word with signs following. Whenever the Word of God was preached, we were taught to expect miracles as surely as night follows day.

2
The Influence of Great Leaders

Dad was pastoring a large church in Covina, California, when Demos Shakarian started the first Full Gospel Business Men's Fellowship meetings. The first meetings were held in Clifton's Cafeteria in Los Angeles, California. Demos Shakarian had a dairy nearby so it was only natural for him to start the meetings in the immediate area.

I was a young teenager at that time, but I still remember quite vividly those first historic meetings of what was to later grow into a worldwide movement of Christian businessmen. Those early meetings left a lasting impression on my life because I was able to fellowship closely with outstanding men of God.

At first, only ten to fifteen men attended the meetings. These few men helped get it started and the attendance grew rapidly. My dad and several other pastors who had strong churches in the area began to get their churches involved in the meetings.

Dad always took me with him to the meetings when he could. We would get up early on Saturday morning and drive all the way from Covina to Los Angeles. The attendance grew in a short while from just a few to around five hundred. I will never forget those powerfully anointed meetings where we gathered in the upper room at Clifton's Cafeteria and raised our hands and praised the Lord.

Some of the best ministers in the nation began coming to minister and give their testimonies. Oral Roberts came to Los Angeles for a crusade and while he was in town, he spoke at the Clifton Cafeteria meetings. Dad was Oral's crusade chairman for the Los Angeles meetings and helped to organize and set up the crusade.

When we went to the Full Gospel Business Men's Fellowship meetings, I always sat at the head of the table with Dad, which meant I was able to sit near and talk with our guest speaker. When Oral Roberts was the guest speaker, I shall never forget how impressed I was at being so near this great man of God and having the privilege of speaking with him. During one of the meetings, he laid his hands on me and prayed for me.

And other great men of God were constantly coming to those early Clifton Cafeteria meetings. Jack Coe, Tommy Hicks, and many outstanding Christian businessmen were guest speakers. How it thrilled me to be able to sit near them, to talk with them, to see and hear them operate in their anointed ministries.

As I associated with those great men of God and heard their testimonies, their messages burned down on the inside of me and motivated me to go out and do something for God. At times it was all I could do to sit still at the table with Dad. I wanted to run out and start preaching on a street corner right then!

Frank Foglio, the master of ceremonies, would often ask me to lead the singing, and I had a chance between songs to exhort a little. At one of the meetings I was so stirred in my spirit that I began praying for the sick between songs, and God healed people. After that, Frank asked me to preach and pray for the sick during the meetings.

About that time Demos Shakarian started a Saturday morning radio program which was broadcast live during the meetings. I will never forget one Saturday morning when Frank asked me to preach and pray for the sick. I was mightily anointed of God and people were healed all over that banquet hall. Everybody was excited. Frank asked me to preach over the radio and to pray for the sick in the radio audience.

The power of God moved into the meeting. People began calling in from the radio audience to testify of their healings. People were shouting and praising God all over the cafeteria. After the radio program was over, Frank asked me to preach again and to pray for the people in the cafeteria for whom we had not had time to pray earlier.

Usually, the main speaker spoke during the radio program and continued to speak after the radio show had ended. But the power of God was so mighty during the services that I ended up speaking three times in one morning. Frank invited me to speak again many times after those marvelous services where God so graciously moved to heal many sick people.

During those early days of the Full Gospel Business Men's Fellowship meetings, I was working for Richard Shakarian, Demos' son, delivering milk for their dairy.

Richard Shakarian and Frank Foglio later set up my crusade in Fontana, California, which made newspaper headlines. Some of Frank's family urged me to preach for them there in Fontana, and Richard and Frank got the big tent and arranged the meetings. Even though I was just twenty-one, I preached each night to a full tent, with people crowded all around the outside. We witnessed many outstanding miracles of healing.

I owe a great deal to Demos Shakarian, Richard Shakarian, Frank Foglio, and the Full Gospel

Business Men's Fellowship. They helped me immensely in my early ministry. Dad and I were with them from the beginning. Dad prayed the dedicatorial prayer over the first issue of *Voice* magazine. Those memories will always be dear to me.

Dad seemed always to be involved with leading men of God. Until he passed away a few years ago, Dad served on Morris Cerullo's executive board as secretary/treasurer. He baptized Jack Coe in water and was with him from the beginning of his ministry.

You can imagine what an influence these great men of God can have on a young person's life. As a young man, I spent much time with some of these ministers — standing beside them while they prayed for the sick, helping them in their meetings, traveling for miles with them from one meeting to another and soaking in the Spirit of God that was in them. Occasionally, some of these men would meet together in a motel room for prayer and I would go with Dad and sit on the floor, drinking in every word as they talked about the things of God.

I am convinced that young people today who desire to develop ministries must spend more time with successful ministries. Some of the spirit of that ministry seems to be imparted to others through close association. I know that is what happened to me. I developed from an awkward kid, too bashful to preach, into an evangelist with a miracle ministry, mainly through close association with great men of God and by sitting under their ministries.

3
Preaching With Jack Coe

We moved from California to Corpus Christi, Texas, where Dad started Bethel Assembly of God Church. I helped him raise up the church and served as minister of youth. Even though I was in full-time ministry, there persisted from deep within me a tremendous drive to go out and conduct great crusades where miracles of healing occurred throughout the audience. Often while ministering to the young people in Dad's church, I would envision myself preaching to masses of people in crusades just as I had seen in the vision when I was only twelve years old.

I could not escape that vision. Always it was before the eyes of my spirit, and always I was reaching for the manifestation of the supernatural in my ministry.

One day Dr. Pierce Brooks called from Dallas and invited me to go with him to a Jack Coe crusade in Birmingham, Alabama. Dr. Brooks put me up in a big hotel and told me I could eat anything I wanted in the restaurant and just sign the ticket.

The room was huge and plush with two big beds. I could have slept in either bed; but for four days and nights during that crusade, I could neither sleep nor eat. I would lie on the floor at night and just cry, unable to stop. The desire to minister locked deep inside me was trying to surface. I cried, not because I was sad or unhappy, but because of the stirring within me by the mighty power of God.

Dr. Brooks was one of the sponsors of that crusade; and since he sat on the platform, I was invited to sit on the platform with him and all the other ministers. When Dr. Brooks stepped up to lead the song service, that huge tent began to echo the praises of God. It sounded like a choir of angels singing. There must have been 10,000 people there, but more were still crowding in. The ushers were asking people to move closer together to make room.

It was an atmosphere of great expectation for the supernatural to begin working. I sat on the platform filled with awe and wonder as the people crowded into the tent. My heart was burning inside. Here I was, only twenty-one years old, and already privileged to associate with these great men of God.

Jack Coe was a big man, both physically and spiritually. He stepped to the microphone and said one word: He shouted, "Hallelujah!" The power of God on that one word shook my whole body and great tears streamed down my face.

"Greater is He (Jesus) that is in me than that cancer that's in you!" Jack Coe would say.

Then he would quote Hebrews 13:8: *Jesus Christ the same yesterday, and to day, and for ever.* Jack quoted that scripture over and over again. Then he would say, "If Jesus ever healed the sick, He can do it again!" Much of Jack's inspiration came from his having attended Smith Wigglesworth's revivals.

The tears continued to flow from my eyes as Brother Coe stepped off the platform and began praying for the people who were lying on stretchers and cots up and down the aisles. Others came to be prayed for in wheelchairs and on crutches. Nearly all were hopeless cases, as far as medical science was concerned.

That night the power of God moved in like a cloud, hovered over the front of the tent, and I saw miracles. Blind eyes were opened. Cripples by the dozens threw down their crutches and walked away. The sick and the dying rose from their stretchers and cots, able to walk home that night.

Jack Coe was as bold as a lion. I had been watching a man in a wheelchair near the front of the platform who seemed to have no control over his muscles. His head bobbed continually from side to side and his arms flopped around when he attempted to move. Brother Coe walked over to this man, took him by the hand, and shouted into the microphone, "Get up, in the name of Jesus!"

The commanding power from Coe's voice shook the audience. It was just as though Jesus were standing there talking with the man. Immediately he got out of the wheelchair and began walking around the tent with his hands in the air, praising God.

As I stood there on the platform, stretching my neck so that I could see everything that was happening, tears streamed down my face profusely, even faster than before. I had seen these great miracles in a vision when I was only twelve; then I thought to myself, *Now I am seeing them with my natural eyes.*

Jack Coe walked down the aisles praying for people, one after another. He would lean over someone on a stretcher and say, "In the name of Jesus, arise and be healed!" And that person would get up and walk away.

If someone seemed to be walking too slowly, he would shout into the microphone, "Run! In the name of Jesus, run!" And the one who had been healed would shout praises to God and begin to run down the aisles of the huge tent.

Occasionally Jack Coe would take crutches away from people and command them to walk in the name of Jesus. They would walk away completely healed, with their crutches tucked under their arms or laid across their shoulders.

Once I saw him slap a bleeding, cancerous sore on a man's forehead. Then he removed his hand to reveal skin completely healed, as clean and white as a baby's.

Jack Coe was a man of miracles. Sitting there on the platform that night so long ago now, I determined in my heart that I would be like that: I would become God's man of miracles. I would heal the sick and break Satan's power over people's lives.

For four days during that crusade I didn't eat a bite. For four nights I didn't sleep in either of those big inviting beds. I left each night when the crusade was over; and in my hunger for the kind of power that Jack Coe had, I began crying out to God. When I returned to that plush hotel room, I fell down on the floor between those soft beds and cried out to God, remaining all night in prayer and communion with Him.

One night after the service Jack Coe asked me to ride down to the local radio station with him where he had to make some tapes. I sat there in the front seat with my head down, not saying anything. I felt unworthy to say a word in the presence of such a man of God.

Jack's mind was on the meeting, I could tell, but he said two things to me that I shall never forget. They are just as clear to me today as that night so long ago when I rode in the car beside him in Birmingham, Alabama.

He turned to me suddenly and said, "Burnie, my church denomination didn't make me what I am."

Then a few minutes later, he said, "Burnie, it doesn't hurt to act like someone else. Elisha acted like Elijah and did twice as many miracles as he did."

That's about all he said all evening. I don't even know why he said what he did, except that God ordained those words to be spoken to me. One thing is for sure: I have never forgotten them.

The two things Jack Coe said to me that night have helped me immensely over the years. The first thing I have always remembered is that my source is God, not man. Jack said that God made him what he was — not his denomination, not man. The second thing I learned was that *I* could do what Jack Coe or any other man has ever done for God, perhaps even more.

This seems to be a principle of the Bible. The prophet Elisha followed in Elijah's footsteps and operated under the same anointing. The disciples followed Jesus; and as apostles in the book of Acts, we find them doing the same miracles Jesus had done and acting just like Jesus had acted.

What Jack Coe had said was that I should not depend on man because the anointing comes from God. However, I can learn a great many things concerning the ministry from anointed men of God. Also, part of the anointing of these great men of God can be transferred to my spirit. **My spirit can receive directly from their spirits.**

On the last day of the crusade, Jack Coe was unexpectedly called out of town and Dr. Pierce Brooks was left in charge of the meeting. Without any warning at all, he called me up to lead the music. There I stood, before a crowd of 7,500 people, with more still coming in.

Leading the song service was easy because the crusade had been going on for six weeks, the people had seen many outstanding miracles, and faith was running high.

I sat down to give the service back to Dr. Brooks, thinking that either he or one of the distinguished preachers on the platform would surely bring the message. Instead Dr. Brooks walked up to the microphone and calmly announced that Rev. Burnie Davis from Corpus Christi, Texas, would bring the message that night.

I walked to the microphone in a state of shock. Having had no idea that I would be speaking, I certainly didn't have a message in mind. My hands were shaking when I took the microphone from Dr. Brooks. He just laid his hand on my shoulder and asked for God's anointing upon me.

I suppose I preached for fifteen or twenty minutes, but I don't know what I preached. To this day I haven't the faintest idea. But I do know that the people seemed to be blessed because they clapped their hands and shouted, "Amen!"

I delivered the short sermon and again turned the service back to Dr. Brooks. He gave a short altar call for the unsaved and had those who responded pray the sinner's prayer. Then he announced that we were going to pray for every person who needed prayer, even if we had to stay there all night. The worst cases, which included those on stretchers and cots, would be prayed for first.

People began lining up for prayer, and I thought I had never seen a healing line so long in my whole life. They brought a chair to the edge of the platform so that someone could sit down and pray for the people as they passed by, as Jack Coe had done.

Satisfied that everything was in order, Dr. Brooks stepped to the microphone and announced, "And now let's raise our hands and praise the Lord as Rev. Burnie Davis comes to pray for the sick."

You could have knocked me over with a feather! Me, a mere twenty-one-year-old kid to pray for hundreds of medically hopeless cases? Me, to follow the great man of God who had been doing mighty miracles night after night in the powerful name of Jesus? Me, Burnie, to follow Jack Coe?

Impossible! I thought. Then I suddenly realized that I had been fasting and praying for those past four days. If I really believed God could use me like that, now was the time to find out.

I walked stiffly to the chair and sat down. I looked into the faces of those sick and broken people — people defeated by Satan, some of them dying. Just then I got mad at the Devil. I remembered the night before when Jack Coe had told me that it didn't hurt to act like someone else. I thought, *Tonight I have preached in Jack Coe's tent. Now I am sitting in his chair about to pray for the sick and dying. I am sitting in his place, so I will just act like Jack Coe and pray for the sick the same way he does.*

As the people were brought by, I leaned over, laid my hands on them, and prayed. The power of God came down and people were getting healed, just as they were when Jack Coe had prayed.

I became electrified by the power of God. The line was moving too slowly, so I jumped off the platform and began to run down the lines of people, praying for them.

I bumped into a cot and the lady on it looked up at me with pleading eyes. When I leaned over and asked what her problem was, she said she was paralyzed from the waist down as a result of having given birth to triplets. She was unable to walk and be a mother to her children and a wife to her husband. I got mad at the Devil for what he had done to her!

I placed both my hands on her head and prayed for her in the name of the Lord Jesus Christ. My hands and entire body were charged with the power of God. I was keenly aware of His mighty power as it left my hands and entered her body.

Right before my eyes, that lady jumped off the cot and began to dance down the sawdust aisle of the tent with her hands lifted as she sang praises to the Lord for her healing. Of course, people all over the tent began shouting praises to God.

Charged with faith and power, I literally ran down that row of cots and stretchers, laying hands on the people and praying for them. Tears streamed down my face as under my breath I gave thanks and glory to God for His having answered my prayer of the past four days and nights.

Someone pulled on my shirtsleeve. "Will you please pray for my daughter?" a woman's voice said. I looked down into the sad eyes of a loving mother. "We have been here four days, waiting for her to be prayed for, and it took us several days to get here. Because she has to take oxygen, it was against the doctor's orders that we checked her out of the hospital. Will you please pray for her?"

I followed the lady to where her daughter was lying on a cot, paralyzed from head to feet. The mother said, "The doctors have given her up. Jesus is her only hope now."

Great compassion flowed out of me toward the young woman lying so still on the cot. I asked the girl if she believed that Jesus would heal her if I laid my hands on her, but she could make no audible reply. All she could do was roll her eyes toward me as an answer.

Stirred with compassion and charged with the power of God, I leaned over the cot and placed my hands upon her head. Her body began to shake under the mighty power of God. Then I stepped back and said, "If you believe that God has healed you, get up and walk. Demonstrate the healing power of God to this great audience tonight. Let them see that the Word of God works now just like it did 2,000 years ago when Jesus walked the earth and demonstrated the power of God."

I spoke boldly into the microphone because I was charged with the power of God and was moving in the world of the supernatural. I was hardly aware of what I was doing. Here I was, a young man barely dry behind the ears, preaching to nearly 10,000 people and acting like I knew what I was doing. But it wasn't just a youth preaching that night; it was a servant of God moving under the mighty anointing of the Holy Spirit. I had stepped out of the world of the natural and into the world of the Spirit of God — and I was enjoying every minute of it!

I was caught up in a supernatural faith, no longer just *believing* for miracles; I *knew* beyond the shadow of a doubt that when I laid my hands on the people, they *would be healed.* With that supernatural power within me, I was simply using my faith to release it upon the people.

I shouted into the microphone, "God has healed this girl who has been totally paralyzed. She is going to walk away from here tonight!"

The girl began struggling to move. The power of God began moving through her body, working with her as she acted out her faith in God's Word. She struggled until she was able to sit up on the edge of the cot. Her mother helped her put on her shoes as she sat there; then, with some help, she stood up beside the cot. Though she was wobbly and needed support to stand, she gained strength by the minute. Then she began to walk — still wobbly, but walking nevertheless. Suddenly, she began to walk normally, displaying greater strength. She walked behind the platform to her husband who was just coming into the tent. The last I saw of them that night, the husband was leading his young wife out of the tent, and the young lady's mother and father were following behind, carrying the cot, the blanket, and the oxygen equipment.

People all over the tent were on their feet, praising God for His healing power!

After praying for the paralyzed girl, I turned around and bumped into a lady who had a tumor in her stomach, so large that it looked as if she were expecting quintuplets. The woman was in great pain and could hardly walk without help.

When I asked if she believed that God would heal her when I laid hands on her, she cried out, "Yes! Yes! I know Jesus will heal me tonight!" I gently placed my hands upon her head, cursed that growth in the name of Jesus, and commanded it to go.

With my own eyes I saw her stomach return to its normal size as the tumor disappeared. Her dress hung loosely around her like an empty feed sack hanging on a nail in a barn.

These are only a few of the mighty miracles I saw that night. Besides these, we counted twenty-four cripples on crutches who were completely healed and five totally blind people whose sight was fully restored. There were a great many healings that we did not count because they were not as evident as the cripples walking, the tumors disappearing, and the blind receiving sight.

A young boy miraculously healed of crippling polio at that Jack Coe crusade in Birmingham, Alabama, came to work years later as a commercial artist and musician in some of our crusades. The young man's name is Nathan Gatch. At the time of this writing he is living in Houston, Texas, where he has a job as a commercial artist and is still working for God.

Until recently, Dr. Pierce Brooks lived in Brazil where he worked as a missionary for a great number of years. We ministered with him in crusades in Brazil on several occasions. Dr. Brooks passed on to be with Jesus in 1981.

Yes, Jesus Christ is *the same yesterday, and to day, and for ever* (Heb. 13:8). His healing power is still available and has not diminished over the years. It is still available to all who will receive it, to all who will release it in their ministries in faith.

4
Six Cents and A Bucketful of Faith

While I was there in Birmingham, Dad wired me to join him in Matamoros, Mexico, where he was conducting a missionary evangelistic crusade in a church. So I left the Jack Coe crusade, full of faith and power, and headed straight for Mexico.

Every night the building was so packed that people stood in the streets waiting to come inside to be prayed for. As I sat on the platform next to Dad, I thought I had never seen so many people packed into a building. They were jammed into the windows and lined up around the walk and in the doorways. Every night hundreds of people were being saved, baptized in the Holy Spirit, and healed.

Dad leaned over and whispered in my ear rather loudly so that the pastor next to him could hear above the loud music, "Son, how would you like to hold a meeting across town? There is a pastor here who would like to have a meeting like this in his church."

"I would be glad to, Dad. When do they want to start, next week?"

Dad and the pastor whispered back and forth for a while; then Dad turned back to me and said, "They want to start tomorrow night. They're going to stay up all night tonight getting handbills ready to pass out so that you will have a good crowd tomorrow night."

It was a church that would seat about one thousand people and they really worked hard the next day spreading the word about that meeting. The church was more than half full the first night. After the service I saw Dad and accused him of sending all his people to my meeting; but he quickly informed me that his crowd hadn't slacked off one little bit. In fact, he said, even more people had attended that night.

"You mean all those people came out just to hear me? Are you sure you didn't send them over?"

Dad just laughed at his novice evangelist, then asked, "Did you read the handbills? Those people didn't come out to hear you, son. They came to get healed."

Every night after our services, Dad and I compared notes on how big the crowds were and how many were saved and healed. I know it was a thrill for Dad to have his son conducting a healing revival in the same town with him.

I shall never forget the first service I preached in Mexico. I stood on the platform facing those people, still living in that spirit of boldness and power that I had experienced in Jack Coe's crusade. I preached on "The Boundless Compassion of Christ," which was a sermon I had found in a book by D. L. Moody.

Filled with love and compassion for the people, I talked about the love of God, the miracles of Christ, and the power of God to heal today. As I preached, I perceived in my spirit that faith began to rise up in the people's hearts. They believed what I was preaching.

After a short sermon, I invited the sick to come forward for prayer. I told them that, no matter what was wrong with them, if they would come up, Jesus would heal them! "Come across the front of the platform one at a time and line up; I am going to pray for you."

Then I grabbed a chair and pulled it up to the edge of the platform just as had been done in the Jack Coe crusade. I also intended to ask each person if they believed God for their healing and what their particular problem was, just as we had done in Birmingham. But when I was properly seated and the first person stood before me, I didn't need to ask about the problem. It was easy to see that the woman was blind. There was only white film where her eyes should have been.

Dear Lord, I thought, *Jack Coe is not here. Oral Roberts is not here. Can we get these blind eyes open without them?*

I decided to move down to the second person in line. "What's wrong with you?" I asked. The interpreter answered, "He is blind!" The third person in line was also blind. I was afraid to go to the fourth! I might find out they were all blind! I bowed my head and began to pray. I was a young man all alone with a building full of people, needing miracles, and none of them spoke my language. Dad wasn't there. Jack Coe wasn't there. Dr. Brooks wasn't there. Nobody was there but Jesus and Burnie Davis.

My heart was filled with compassion for those poor sick people. I knew that for most of them I was the only hope they had. With tears streaming down my face, I lifted my hands and prayed, "Jesus, anoint these hands and make them healing hands. Confirm Your Word among these people tonight. Do not, O Lord, confirm the words of Burnie Davis, the inexperienced boy, but confirm Your Word which has been spoken by Your servant tonight."

Here goes, Lord, I thought, as I motioned for the first lady to be brought before me again. I laid my hands upon her head and placed both thumbs over her unseeing eyes, just as I had seen Oral Roberts do. Then I commanded the blind spirit to come out of her in the name of Jesus. As I prayed, I became charged with the power of God. I reached that point of knowing beyond a shadow of a doubt that the miracles *would* occur.

I removed my hands and bent over to look straight into her blind eyes. I wanted to see the miracle take place. The interpreter and the pastor were standing there with the lady, watching with me. As I looked into her eyes, the white film began to melt away. The film dissolved until we could see her pupils and complete eyeballs clearly. The lady began to dance, shouting, "I can see! I can see!" When we calmed her down, she read a poster on the wall of the church.

The pastor, the interpreter, and the whole audience went wild, and I went wild with them! I jumped off the platform and ran up and down the aisles, with the pastor right behind me!

That experience did something for me. I knew God was with *me* — Burnie Davis. Previously, the miracles that occurred in my ministry were while I was preaching in the presence of great men of God. I had always wondered if those miracles had been sent by God because of their faith. But this time, I was all alone with God. No great men of faith were there with me.

That night, the rest of the people were easy to pray for. I just laid my hands on their heads and watched the miracles take place. As the blind eyes quickly opened, I was wishing they were all blind!

Praise God, the Word works! Act on God's Word and it will work! But act in faith, boldly!

A man stood before me, stooped over at a 45-degree angle. I reached out, touched him on the head, and thanked Jesus for his healing. Suddenly, the same Spirit and anointing that had rested upon Jack Coe came upon me. I was mad at the Devil for what he had done to this man. I jumped down off the platform, stood behind the man, and jammed my knee into his back. Reaching down, I grabbed his shoulders and straightened him up as I commanded Satan to set him free.

Crack! It sounded like every bone in that man's back had broken. There was such a shocked silence in that auditorium, you could have heard a pin drop. The babies weren't even crying.

The funny thing was that I was shocked, too. I thought, *You crazy fool, what have you done now?* I had jumped down and grabbed that man without realizing what I was doing.

Suddenly, fear gripped me as I stood there before that audience. For a split second, I was frozen with fear. Then I remembered what Dad had said: "Faith is the opposite of fear, and fear is a spirit you must deal with."

"Fear, go in the name of Jesus!" I commanded. Just as suddenly as it had departed, faith returned to me again. I grabbed the man by the collar, pulled him up, then pushed him up and down several times. Faith moved through the audience and the people began clapping their hands again.

The man stood up perfectly straight before me with his hands raised, praising God, and with big tears streaming down his face.

I stopped him as he started to walk away and asked if he had felt any pain when I straightened him up.

"No," he exclaimed. "I never felt a thing when you prayed for me."

I mention what happened with this man because it was a lesson I learned. You see, Satan lied to me and tried to destroy me. I had acted in faith, under the anointing of God; but Satan tried to put fear on me by telling me I had missed God and had broken the man's back. But, praise God, the man didn't feel a thing. God had performed surgery on his back without even giving him an anesthetic, and he never felt a pain!

That same night, a lady came running to the altar when I presented the invitation for salvation. After she had repeated the sinner's prayer, she fell backwards and lay quietly on the floor. Though her lips were moving, no audible words came forth. I felt impressed that she was having a vision. After the service, I talked with her through the interpreter.

She said that she had seen Jesus walking toward her with His hands cupped. When Jesus drew nearer to her, she saw that His hands were filled with blood and she knew that it was His own blood. Then she said that Jesus reached down on the inside of her and washed her with His own blood.

"And now I feel so clean," she said. Her face shone like the face of an angel.

This was my first experience preaching on the mission field. We saw a great many outstanding miracles during that crusade. Rev. Ray Morelock, an Assembly of God missionary, attended the crusade, then approached me afterwards about ministering in Mexico for a while. He made up an itinerary for me to preach from one end of Mexico to the other. I was to go home and prepare for the trip; then return within a few weeks to begin the campaign.

I was so fired up that the thought of how such an undertaking would be financed never crossed my mind. Finances are a very real and necessary part of the ministry, and it was through this experience that I learned a good lesson about finances.

My young wife Dolly and I drove to California to leave our new baby with Dolly's parents while we were in Mexico. Then we returned to Corpus Christi, where I had been working with Dad as pastor of youth, so that we could pack and prepare for our extended preaching tour through Old Mexico. I knew we would be gone for several months if we followed Brother Morelock's itinerary.

Brother Morelock had even arranged for an interpreter — Maria Selapas, a Spanish schoolteacher in Brownsville, Texas, who would make the 9,000-mile trip with us. Our schedule was to preach every night and sometimes several times during the day.

Both Dolly and I knew in our spirits that we were going but, in the natural we didn't know how. When we returned from California, I checked the cash in my pocket. It wasn't difficult to count; there was exactly six cents. But we knew it was God's will that we go and that He would provide. So, by faith, we began packing and preparing for the trip. There was a Full Gospel Business Men's meeting in town that morning which I felt urged in my spirit to attend, so Dolly elected to stay home and finish packing.

Before the meeting I told some of the leaders about my trip and asked if they would pray for us during the service. I was asked to come to the front and tell about the crusade we had just closed in Mexico and about the trip we were going on. I spent about five minutes telling about the many miracles of healing we had seen and concluded by saying that we would be leaving that evening to return to Mexico.

In my heart I was believing for a financial miracle. I thought perhaps they would take an offering that would end our financial problems. But I learned some important lessons way back there when I was just starting out: God is your source, not man, and sometimes you have to walk your faith to the end.

They didn't take an offering nor was anything mentioned about helping us financially. I stood at the door after the meeting, shaking hands with well-wishers for our missionary trip, but no one offered any money. When just about everyone had gone, an old man walked by, hugged me, and pressed a bill into my hand.

I stood there in the doorway for a few minutes holding the bill, not wanting to look down. I was thinking, "Praise God, maybe this is a thousand-dollar bill. It must be!"

When the last person had left, I walked through the lobby of the motel where the meeting had been held. I stopped long enough to unroll the crumpled bill and look at it. My heart was pounding so that I was sure my tie was flopping up and down in rhythm with my heart.

I looked down quickly at the wrinkled bill, then looked again to make sure. The old man had given me a five-dollar bill. I stood there in the lobby for a moment thinking. I was not discouraged. I only knew that God had another way, a better way.

I remembered what Raymond T. Richey had done when he was a boy. His dad had taught him to believe God for anything. Once he and his father were on their way to a revival meeting and had run out of gasoline. There were no houses around, let alone gas stations, so Raymond jumped out of the car and started running up and down the side of the road.

"What are you doing, son?" old Dad Ritchey called out.

"Don't worry, Dad. I'm looking for a can or something that will hold water." He found a rusty can and filled it with muddy water from a ditch.

When his dad wanted to know why they needed muddy water, Raymond explained that water was the only thing available. Jesus had turned water into wine when there was no more wine, so they would simply ask Jesus to turn water into gasoline.

When Raymond filled the tank with muddy water, his father dared not rebuke him. After all, he had been the one to teach Raymond to use faith based on the Word of God.

They filled the gas tank, prayed, and drove to the revival meeting. The motor never missed one time! *God is a God of miracles.*

As I thought about that story, my faith began to rise. I also remembered the time my brother and I had run out of gasoline late at night sixty-five miles from home on a lonely highway. We stood beside the car, joined hands, and set our faith in agreement for a miracle. We drove sixty-five miles home on an empty gas tank and faith in God's Word.

The Word of God works; it never fails. I knew that if I had to, I could go 9,000 miles on five dollars and six cents.

I started toward the door with my faith in high gear when I heard, "Burnie! Oh, Burnie!"

I turned quickly to see Guy Brazelton standing in the lobby grinning at me.

"Hey, Burnie, come have lunch with me. What do you say?"

"I had better not, Guy. Dolly is packed and waiting for me. We are headed for Mexico today."

"Yeah, I know," he said. "Call her and tell her you will be a little late. Here's a dime."

We sat down at a table and, before the waitress had time to take our order, Guy looked straight at me and asked, "Burnie, do you have any money?"

"Yeah, sure, I have, Guy," I replied. I wasn't lying. I had exactly five dollars and six cents.

Then he looked straight into my eyes, and his next question got me: "How much do you have, Burnie?"

I returned his eye contact. I looked straight at him and, with all the pride I could muster, said, "I have five dollars and six cents."

With eyes filled with tears, Guy said, "Burnie, the Lord had me turn around on my way home this morning and come back to look for you. I knew in my spirit that you had a financial need." He pulled out his checkbook, wrote a check for $250, and said, "I'm sorry, I don't have much cash on me. If you will let me know where you're going to be in Mexico, I will wire you some money."

On my way home, God impressed me to stop by a friend's office to tell him where we were going and why. He gave me a check for $150, then went to an empty desk and pulled out a check for $50 written by an employee who wasn't even there that day.

I ended up with $450 cash to begin the trip, and God supplied the rest of the money as we needed it.

Again I say, *God is a God of miracles.* He is our source, and His Word works. The Word of God will never fail!

At any time I could have yielded to discouragement and canceled the trip. In the natural I had a perfect excuse for doing so.

I think that's the reason many who are called never make it in the ministry. They so yield to circumstances that those circumstances become the governing force in their lives. But God is not moved by circumstances. God is a faith God, and He is moved only by our uncompromising faith in His Word.

Dolly and I made that 9,000-mile trip through Old Mexico, seeing many outstanding miracles of healing and deliverance. A great many unbelievers who saw those miracles believed on the Lord Jesus Christ and were saved. It was like another chapter in the book of Acts.

This missions trip to Mexico was only the beginning of a miracle ministry which has expanded tremendously through the years, affecting many thousands of lives throughout the United States, Latin America, India, Canada, and the British West Indies.

5
Fast Bullets and Nighttime Witches

In the Armeria, Colima crusade in Mexico, I met the Devil head on.

The people of Armeria, Colima were held in bondage by witchcraft. They had been told not to believe what we were preaching in our crusade, or they would be severely punished by the gods. People were attending the meetings, but would not respond to the ministering of the Word.

Evidently the local witches were afraid that they were losing their hold on the people because at our meeting one night a witch showed up to oppose us.

Our platform was located on one edge of an old bullring, and most of the people were seated on the sides and in front of me. There were bleachers behind me, but these, for the most part, were unoccupied.

I had just stepped up to the podium to deliver the message burning in my heart when I felt in my spirit that the people were suppressed. Every word I spoke seemed to bounce off the stone walls of the arena and come back to me. The people even appeared to be sitting lower on the bleachers, as if they didn't want to be seen.

On impulse, I turned around on the platform and looked behind me. Directly behind me was the most vicious-eyed woman I have ever seen. Her long gray hair was matted and straggly. Her eyes were glazed and seemed to be staring right through me.

Chanting, she lit sparklers, then whirled them about while doing a little dance on the bleachers.

The people became really attentive, watching every move I made. They greatly feared the witch. During each meeting I had been preaching that Jesus Christ's power is stronger than the Devil's. **This was the real test for them.**

I turned to look again at the old witch. She had two cigars, one in either corner of her mouth, gripped tightly between her rotted teeth. I smelled a horrible odor, that of burning chicken feathers.

The witch began dipping feathers in a pot near her feet, then flicking the feathers, throwing liquid from the pot toward me. A low moan burst forth from the audience; then a hush fell. I knew that they thought this was the end for me.

I looked around the bullring. A rifle shot could ring out from the darkness at any moment, and it surely *would be* the end. Such things had happened!

The power of Satan became so strong, I could have cut it with a knife. I looked at my team members for help, but they were only looking at me with open mouths. None of them had ever before experienced anything like this.

What was I to do? I knew some of the people in the meeting believed strongly in the power of witchcraft. If I simply ignored the old lady, which I was tempted to do, those who believed in the witch would convince themselves that she had won. In that case we might as well pack up and go home. On the other hand, if I rebuked her, I could well be signing my own death warrant. Someone, or several people, could be watching with a gun to protect her.

I bowed my head and prayed silently: "Father, in the name of Your blessed Son, Jesus, I cannot allow the Devil to make a public display of himself in front of all these people. Jesus, help me now, I pray."

Caught up in the realm of the supernatural, I turned suddenly toward the old witch, who was dancing and chanting curses toward me. I pointed the index finger of my right hand at her ugly face and stepped toward her. While the audience let out a loud gasp, fearing for my safety and theirs, I addressed the demonic force within the witch: "Satan, I rebuke you in the name of Jesus! I bind you from further interference in this meeting. I've put up with you too long. I break your power over this people."

The old witch, who had been dancing and twisting her body in all types of weird contortions, wilted down like a wet noodle and slumped over the bleacher; then she lay in a motionless heap.

Suddenly, the people came alive. They went wild when they realized that they need not fear the witches of the city. They knew the Christ I preached had more power than the local coven of witches. Hundreds came running to the front for salvation that night. Over thirty-five people were healed of tumors. One lady had a growth in her stomach the size of a football. As the audience watched, the growth disappeared, leaving her dress to hang loosely about her body.

The old witch didn't die, but she lay quietly on the bleachers until after the service when team members witnessed to her. One of the team members, Terry Mize, tells about the crusade:

"As Brother Davis preached, you could feel the expectation of the people. As he delivered the message that God had laid on his heart, miracles began to happen. Tumors and growths disappeared. Blind eyes opened; deaf ears unstopped; joints and limbs began to receive life; miracle after miracle took place.

"I remember one case, a young mother who came to the front with tears streaming down her face. She told me that while Brother Davis was preaching, she saw that her three-year-old twins, who had been deaf all their lives, suddenly were able to hear. Brother Davis tested their hearing, and God received the glory because they were perfectly healed.

"One boy about twelve years old had never been able to speak; God healed him. There were countless others. What a joy it is to watch someone who has been blind all his life begin to see lights and people, and to hear him cry out, 'I can see! I can see!'

"We were especially amused with one man who was selling corn-on-the-cob. He was healed of arthritis during the services. When Brother Davis said, 'Check yourself; examine yourself; make sure God has healed you. Then come up and give Him the glory,' hundreds of people streamed forward. The corn vendor bent over and checked himself, but was afraid to leave his business to come testify. As soon as he had hidden his money to start forward, a customer would come and he would have to go back. Finally, on the last night with real determination he came and told what God had done for him. Multitudes of lost souls were born into the Kingdom of God during the crusade. The city will never be the same again."

6
Angels As The Wind

"He (God) makes winds his messengers . . ." (Ps. 104:4 NIV).

In speaking of the angels the Apostle Paul says, "He (God) makes his angels winds" (Heb. 1:7 NIV).

Far below us, winding through the tall trees and jungle growth like thread through a needle, flowed the river. Leading away from the river were trails and paths to tiny Mexican villages, the targets of our "bombing" mission.

"Okay, bombadier, get ready!" shouted David Slack, our pilot, as he guided his red and white Cherokee aircraft away from the river and into a circle around a village.

Below us the villagers grew larger and the grass huts came into plain view as we continued to descend. Hearing the plane, the residents of this tiny village, hidden from the world (but not from God) in the thick darkness of the jungle, ran from their houses and from the fields, all eyes looking upward at the strange giant bird hovering so near.

Ruben Ramirez — an attorney, interpreter, and our National evangelist and promoter — broke open a fresh package of "bombs" and handed them over the seat to me.

To achieve success, "bombing" missions must be planned to absolute perfection. Flying at low altitudes in these mountains and jungle areas could mean instant death. The slightest mistake, miscalculated wind velocity, or unforeseen air pocket (actually huge vacuums caused by changes in air pressure) could cause the small plane to drop like a rock, being smashed to pieces on the rocks and trees below.

The possibility always exists that unfriendly inhabitants of the villages might fire on the plane with high-powered rifles. This has happened in the past. As a result of Communist guerrilla infiltration into the remote villages, or *panchos* as they are called, it is becoming extremely difficult to work in these areas, and great caution must be used.

As David circled the plane over the treetops, we could see the villagers, like scampering midgets, running and waving their hands excitedly, while men in the plowed fields were leaving their oxen and running through crooked rows at breakneck speed to get to their village for the exciting event. In this remote region where a radio is a great treasure and a trip into a city is a once-in-a-lifetime (if ever) accomplishment, an airplane buzzing the village is one of life's big thrills.

David pulled the plane into an incredibly steep bank at precisely the right moment, allowing for wind drift and altitude. One wing pointed upward toward God, the other downward toward the creation of His hands and the object of His love.

"Now! Bombs away!" David screamed.

For a split second I looked straight down through the open window at the brown-skinned people below.

"Father, in the name of Jesus, anoint Your Word to their hearts," I prayed. Then I let the "bombs" slide through my hands downward to the excited villagers.

Our "bombs" were the Gospel of John and announcements of our forthcoming crusade in a nearby city. As the booklets tumbled crazily through the air, tossing in the prop wash, the villagers scattered like ants on an anthill, trying desperately to catch the precious Gospels before they hit the ground.

David quickly pulled the light plane back so that the wings were level, then opened the throttle and raised the flaps. Through the still-open window I could see the people and houses become smaller, then disappear in the distance as the aircraft burrowed into a thick mountain of fluffy white clouds.

"*Vaya con Dios.* God go with you," I said.

"Amen," Ruben replied from the back seat.

David climbed to 2,500 feet, then leveled off as we headed downriver for the next village.

It was customary on each planned bombing mission to drop Gospels in as many villages as our supply would allow. We bombed six additional villages along the river, and then headed home to our hotel room in Veracruz to pray and otherwise prepare for our large crusade in the ball parks of the city the next day.

With the bombing missions completed for the day, we began noticing the breathtaking beauty of the great river below us. The water was peaceful and calm, and the jungle seemed to fold over into the river along the banks. Huge lily pads with bright red and white flowers floated on the crystal-clear water.

"Let's go down a little closer and take a look," Dave suggested.

It was against my better judgment, but I could not resist, anymore than Dave, the temptation to survey this wondrous beauty of God's handiwork. So down we went to within fifty or sixty feet of the great body of water. At this close range, we could see the fish jumping in the water.

"Quick, Dave, hand me your camera," I said.

I pointed the camera toward the river and pushed the button, but nothing happened.

"Hey, Dave, how do you take a picture with this thing anyway?" I asked in disgust at having missed a beautiful scene.

Dave quickly showed me how to turn the film to another picture, then we both looked up at the same time. Across the river directly in front of us stretched three federal power lines as large around as my index finger. It was too late! We were right upon the lines and could go neither over them nor under them.

"Oh, my God, help us!" David screamed as we flew right into the ominous high voltage lines which were supported on either bank by gigantic trees and buried within the jungle.

"Oh, God, we need a miracle," I prayed as the wires popped against the plane. The windshield shattered and sparks flew everywhere. For a split second, we seemed suspended in air; then the plane headed down, toward the dense jungle on the left bank of the river.

I have heard that your whole life passes before your eyes in a brief second when you face death, but I was too busy praying and trying to figure out how to stay alive.

In a split second of breath, I screamed out, "Dave, don't land in the trees, man! Set her down in the water! We'll have a chance in the river!"

Then Ruben spoke up from the back seat in his slow English drawl. "Brother, is the wing supposed to be like that?"

David and I both popped our heads toward the wing where Ruben was pointing. The aileron had been knocked loose on the left wing and stood straight up, seven or eight feet from the wing. That was the reason the plane was flying so drastically to the left.

"Oh, God, help us!" David prayed. "We've got to get this plane on the ground."

"Set it in the river," I repeated. Neither of us knew what to do.

David tried to turn the plane away from the left bank of the river just before we were about to hit the trees. Miraculously, the left wing lifted and David headed back over the river.

"Thank You, Jesus, for a miracle!" we all prayed.

David said, "Burnie, I've got to set it down in the river."

"You're still flying, David. Look for an open field," I screamed out in a high, shrill voice.

After a minute or two, the plane was still flying over the river without dipping back to the left bank.

"I'm going to check it out and see what kind of control we have," David ventured.

"Man, whatever you do, be careful," I advised, looking toward the thick jungle on both sides of the river and suddenly wondering how big the alligators grew there.

David eased the plane to a higher altitude and found that he had perfect control when he turned in either direction. All three of us began shouting and praising God for a mighty miracle. David flew on to a small airport some fifteen minutes away. When we approached the airport, we decided not to change airspeed, since we weren't sure that the plane would fly at more than one speed. We landed with flaps up in excess of 140 miles per hour.

"Thank You, Jesus, for another miracle!" we yelled.

Once on the ground again, we inspected the plane. The prop was badly damaged; the aileron was completely turned away from the wing on one end. There were cuts and gashes everywhere in the wings, tail, and body. Even the gas cap was missing.

It was aerodynamically impossible for the plane to fly in that condition. But, praise God, the angels came *as the wind* and bore up the wings of that little red and white plane. **God is still in the business of performing miracles for His children.**

Once we were on the ground again and safe, we faced new dangers. It is against the national laws of Mexico to run a plane through federal power lines, so we were in danger of having the plane confiscated by the federal government. Even as we inspected the plane, we saw soldiers approaching from a distance.

Fortunately, the manager of the airport had been converted in one of our crusades and was a good friend and Christian brother. "Quick," he urged, "take off the broken aileron and cover the plane with this canvas." He then hurried us away from the airport in his car just before the soldiers arrived. We looked back and noticed them discussing our plane, but we did not hear from them again.

We still do not know what the Christian airport manager told them about our plane; but we do know that God performed another miracle for us just when it was needed.

God's angels revealed themselves to us *as the wind* on another occasion when we were on "bombing" missions in the high mountain areas of Mexico. We had flown over a mountain range, perhaps 10,000 feet in elevation, and had entered a valley where our target city was located. God had placed a great burden on our hearts for this city.

Many missionaries had been driven out of it at gunpoint and warned never to come back or they would be killed. How our hearts burned within us as the wings of our plane tipped over this city of thousands who had never even heard the name of Jesus Christ mentioned.

How privileged we felt that God had chosen us to reach these seemingly unreachable people with the Gospel of Jesus Christ. Our spirits witnessed with God's Holy Spirit that it was God's time for the people of this city to receive His miracle power and to learn about Jesus, so we began preparing to drop our gospel tracts and announcements of a forthcoming crusade.

As the plane entered the valley, we lowered the flaps about ten percent, decreased airspeed to eighty, and entered a tight circle around the city.

David Rice opened a window and began bombing the city with tracts on salvation and healing. Thousands of tracts floated through the air and the eager people were scrambling and running to grab the tiny bits of paper even before they hit the ground.

We were flying so low that we had to fly around the steeple on the Catholic church which was right in the center of the city. Over to the right of the city was a small airstrip. We noticed a Volkswagen parked in the center of the strip and a man, standing in front of it, holding a rifle. Quickly we flew away to get out of rifle range.

We gained altitude and headed back toward the mountain range.

"David," I said, "the Lord has just impressed me to go back. We need to bind the powers of Satan over this city and loose it to receive the gospel message."

"Amen! Amen!" David said, excitedly agreeing with me.

The Bible mentions *the prince of the power of the air* (Eph. 2:2), and I have learned that cities and countries can have evil spirits controlling them and preventing their reception of the Gospel. Before the people can be reached successfully in such cases, these evil spirits must be dealt with.

David and I had an old-fashioned prayer meeting inside the cockpit of our little plane as we chased devils from that city. We could sense the mighty power of God as we commanded devils to release it and claimed a mighty victory for God.

We moved from village to village on our way back toward the mountains. Suddenly, I glanced down at my air speed indicator and nearly froze with panic. "Airspeed 70!" I shouted at David. I had been pulling the stick back without realizing it, and had been in a gradual climb since leaving the city. So intent had we been on accurately bombing the villages that we had not noticed the gentle climb toward the mountain range which now loomed before us like impassable sentinels.

"We're in a box canyon!" David shouted above the roar of the engine. "We can't turn around in here. Not enough room."

The plane was flying at full power with flaps at ten degrees and airspeed seventy. It couldn't climb at any faster rate without stalling out. On either side of us loomed tall pine trees on the steep walls of the mountains. We had no room to turn, and the mountains were too steep to climb over. We had no choice but to continue straight ahead at our present speed and rate of climb. The mountains were far above us and, as we flew nearer, we could see tall pine trees on the tops of the mountains.

"Pray, David!" I said. "Man, if you have *ever* prayed, pray now!"

Dear God, I thought to myself, *here I am, an inexperienced pilot with only 100 hours of flying time, down here in this wilderness trying to work for You. I can't climb any faster because, if I reduce speed, the plane will go into a stall. If You want me to continue to work for You, God, You've got to send a miracle and send one quickly!*

My heart pained and my palms became sticky with cold, clammy sweat. David was praying intently, almost under his breath, so as not to disturb me. Both David and I became deadly silent as we bore straight toward the mountains and trees, looming like giant shadows of doubt before us.

We came so near that I could clearly make out the bark on the pine trees, and we were headed right into them.

"Father, in the name of Jesus, send a mighty miracle wind. I decree a miracle wind *now,* in the name of Jesus!"

I gripped the stick tightly as the words seemed to rise out of my spirit and flow forth from my lips.

"Thank You for deliverance, Father, in the name of Jesus," David prayed with uplifted hands and tears in his eyes.

Our wheels were inches away from the topmost branches of the pines on the mountain slope. There was no possibility of making it over the giant pines on the mountain peak, which now stood only a few hundred feet in front of us.

Suddenly, there was a whistling sound in the trees and the branches began to sway. A hard wind was blowing toward us from over the mountain, enough to lift our little Cessna 182 right over the tops of those giant pine trees! Up and over the mountain peak we went. I headed the nose of the plane down to pick up airspeed.

"Thank You, Father! Praise You, Jesus! Praise God! Praise God!" we cried.

"Burnie," David said, looking back at the pines on the top of the mountain, "now do you want to know the color of that bird's eyes in the pine tree back there?"

We both enjoyed a hearty laugh and continued to rejoice and praise God as we headed down the mountain range and home to our hotel.

"All in a day's work," the experienced bush pilots might tell you; but for me, I am convinced that God sent His angels in the form of the wind to lift our plane over the mountain.

Back in my hotel room that night, the Devil woke me with great fear. I sat on the side of my bed in a clammy sweat, trembling with fear as I realized what a close call we had had, and how I would have to fly out again into the mountains the next day. I wrestled with satanic fear most of the night, but God strengthened me and gave me complete victory over the fear of flying.

The next day was a beautiful day for flying, and for praising God.

7
Will God Ever Come To San Pedro Sula?

Circling our plane over San Pedro Sula, the second largest city of Honduras, something strange caught our attention. I banked to the right, then dropped for a closer look.

"Something's not right here," I said, pointing to a huge red mountain, projecting like an angry festering boil out of the thick green jungle growth on the edge of the city.

"Can you go down for a closer look?" asked Terry Mize, one of our team members.

Flying lower, we could see the tops of houses, automobiles, buses, and trucks protruding from the thick, red mud. It was obvious that there had been a devastating avalanche and that several villages and a part of San Pedro Sula had been buried beneath the red shroud.

After landing our plane at the local airport, we were soon to learn firsthand what a demoralizing effect this catastrophe had on the residents of that lovely city.

A great deal of preparation goes into a crusade as big as the one we had planned for San Pedro Sula. For several weeks National pastors had been working to get prayer support from their churches and to inform as many people as possible by distributing handbills and by word of mouth.

The next day was a busy one for me. Although permits from the local government had already been secured, there was still much work to be done.

While visiting the local utilities office to secure a permit for electricity, I noticed how sad everyone seemed. Then again at the local television station where we went to announce our crusade, everyone was talking about the recent avalanche which had caused so many deaths and left so many homeless and a great number injured and crippled for life. At the radio station also, I was met with the same wall of depression and heavy sadness.

Later, at the newspaper office, people cried as they talked about "the terrible punishment from God," as they called it. I had gone to the newspaper to take out full-page advertisements of our meetings and to have them write a news story on the coming crusade.

The newspaper personnel could not believe I would do such a thing. To their thinking, it would be sacrilegious for me to run a full-page ad with the headlines, "Jesus Saves And Heals." The people had been told by the local clergy that the avalanche was God's way of punishing them for their sins. They had been made to believe that their problem was caused by God.

I attempted to witness to them about the mercy of God in sending His only Son Jesus to die for our sins, but they could not hear what I was saying because of their own grief.

As I attempted to tell the printer about the love of Jesus, he only sobbed out, "My own son and little daughter died in the terrible punishment."

Determined to do all within my power to bring the love and joy of God to this city of sadness, I arranged to have huge banners printed with the words, "Jesus Saves And Heals." We would stretch the gigantic banners across every major street in San Pedro Sula.

Early the next morning while on my way to breakfast at the hotel restaurant, I stopped to buy a paper from an old black man seated near the entrance. He appeared to be paralyzed on one entire side of his body. On his lap laid a trumpet neatly wrapped in a cloth. I handed him a flier announcing our crusade; but when he read it, he began to shake his head violently. Although he spoke English, understanding him was difficult because of his paralytic condition. He could use only one side of his mouth when speaking; and as he talked, saliva drooled down his chin. When I could not understand him, he simply pointed to the flier and shook his head vigorously.

I entered the restaurant where the other team members were waiting for our regular morning meeting. There was not the usual light talk and laughter this morning. Although I attempted to steer the conversation away from the recent devastation, that seemed to be the only topic on everyone's mind.

Terry said, "When we picked up the lumber to finish the platform, there was a poor man there who had lost his wife and six children. I tried to witness to him, but he couldn't understand how God could love him and allow that to happen to his family."

Most of the others had similar experiences in attempting to witness to the local people. I shifted the conversation back to the work at hand. We were scheduled to begin the meeting in two days and much work yet remained. Everyone assured me that everything would be ready by the end of the next day, which was the night the crusade would begin. I wanted to clear my mind of details so that I could spend the next two days in prayer for the crusade that night.

As we walked out of the restaurant together, we stopped in front of the black man who was selling newspapers. One of the local pastors with us explained that the old man had once been a leading musician in San Pedro Sula. He had played his trumpet for all the major festivities and was well known by all the townspeople. He had suffered several strokes and had been almost completely paralyzed for many years. His family members were killed in the recent avalanche. Now he was all alone.

Actually, there were quite a few black people living in Honduras. Many of their ancestors had been brought in from Jamaica by owners of large plantations.

The old man was still holding the flier of our meeting which I had given him. When the local pastor began witnessing to him about the love of Jesus, the old man only shook his head, mumbling something in Spanish and in English.

"What is he saying?" I asked, leaning closer to him.

"He is saying, 'No! No! God will never come to San Pedro Sula! He will never come here because we are a wicked people and His wrath is turned on us!'"

The old man looked up at us with the saddest eyes I have ever seen. My heart was drawn toward him with the compassion of Christ. I wanted desperately to help him, and all the others in San Pedro Sula. But how were we to reach beyond the great wall of despair, fear, and grief which surrounded them?

I saw the old man several times during the day as I went about attending to last minute details, such as securing permits to hang our banners over the streets and locating someone to drive through the streets and announce our meeting over a loudspeaker. I could not seem to get that old man off my mind, and occasionally tears filled my eyes as I prayed, "Jesus, help that old man and the people of this city. Let them see Your glory, O Lord."

That night, our last free night before the crusade, I called a prayer meeting in the hotel for all the team workers. The local pastors were meeting with their churches for an all-night prayer meeting.

A spirit of depression seemed to have hold on the entire city. There was much negative talk among the local pastors, and some were even in favor of canceling the crusade. They did not feel that we would get much participation in the meetings.

Sleep would not come to me that night. I tossed and turned in my bed, then finally gave up and dressed for a stroll. At that late hour most of the streets around the hotel were deserted.

San Pedro Sula was a beautiful old city, typically Latin American. The buildings were white, and huge trees lined the streets. The city was surrounded by mountains covered with a tropical jungle growth. Bananas, mangoes, and other fruits grew wild. The jungles were teeming with wild parrots and monkeys.

Walking down the narrow streets, I heard the trees rustle as a cool breeze began to blow. The tree limbs swayed in the breeze and made dancing shadows beneath the street lamps. It was almost as if these shadows were mocking me. They seemed to say, "You will see no miracles in San Pedro Sula. There will be no mighty miracles here, and the people will laugh at you because you said they would be healed."

Out of the darkness beyond the street lights I felt a spirit of fear approach me. Goose bumps paraded down my spine and up the back of my neck.

I remembered my dad warning me about fear just before a big crusade. One of his favorite scriptures was 2 Timothy 1:7: *For God hath not given us the spirit of fear; but of power, and of love, and of a sound mind.*

"Remember, son, faith is the opposite of fear," Dad used to say. "Fear is a spirit from Satan, and you can do something about it. Speak to fear and command it to go, in the name of Jesus. If you allow it to hang around, fear will destroy your faith. If you allow that to happen, you might as well pack up and go home."

"Thank you, Dad," I said under my breath. I began rebuking the spirit of fear and depression from my mind. Dad had never had a failure. His meetings had always been tremendously successful. I was determined not to meet my Waterloo at San Pedro Sula.

Immediately realizing the strategy of Satan, I stood tall, squared my shoulders, gritted my teeth, and chewed out the Devil for trying to kill the people of this city and then deceive them into believing that God had done it to them. My blood began to boil as I thought about the old paralyzed black man shaking his head and declaring that God would not dare come to his city. I shook my fist at the Devil and commanded him to loose his hold on the people of San Pedro Sula.

8
God Came To San Pedro Sula!

Several hours before the meeting was scheduled to start, I began praying for God's anointing. As was my custom before the opening night of a crusade, I did not eat that day. I paced back and forth in my small hotel room, praying in my heavenly language and yielding myself completely to God.

My mind was not on how many people may or may not be there, or how many miracles I might see. I knew God had sent me to San Pedro Sula for one purpose: that the people might see Jesus, and that through Him the works of Satan might be destroyed.

While yielding myself completely to God, the anointing began to come upon me. Faith — the God-kind of faith — began to tug at my heart. In my spirit I saw a dark cloud hovering over the city of San Pedro Sula. Beneath that cloud were thousands of sad, lonely, and depressed people. I saw the crippled and the homeless — people in agony and despair. Then as I continued to pray, the cloud began to move away and the sun shown down over the city. In the bright sunshine were thousands of bright smiling faces. There was great joy throughout the city and surrounding villages as the people lifted their hands in praise to God.

While the vision was passing before my eyes, a tremendous peace and joy began to fill my own spirit. Then I laughed in a holy laughter as the Holy Spirit ministered through me. I was interceding for a city and I knew that God had heard my prayer. The answer was on the way.

That night I rode with one of the team members to the open field where the meeting was in progress. When the song service was over, I got out of the car and walked with the team members to the platform. As I climbed upon the huge platform, the people began singing, "Only believe. Only believe. All things are possible. Only believe."

A choir, made up of members from the local churches, was on the platform. As their voices rang out over the extensive loudspeaker system, I was sure people for miles around must have heard the beautiful singing.

The platform, constructed of heavy planks, stood about shoulder high to an average man. About thirty feet wide and forty feet long, it was constructed so as to allow plenty of room for people who had been healed to gather and testify of their healings. Also, its size and height provided protection from the crowds. Occasionally, when miracles begin to take place in meetings, the people become so excited that they rush against the platform. If it is not strong enough to withstand the force of thousands of bodies pushing against it, many injuries can result.

I walked to one corner of the platform, knelt and prayed. I did not look to see how many people were there. My faith was not based on circumstances, but on God's Word. I knew God had sent me there to do His work and now it was all in His hands.

When the choir had finished singing, the interpreter introduced me to the people in Spanish. I arose from prayer and walked to the podium. Laying my Bible down on it, I stood looking out over the people. There were probably not more than 1,000 people there — a very small crowd for a crusade in Latin America. Also, from the way the people were singing, I knew this crowd mostly represented members of the local churches.

Looking out over the people that first night would have been discouraging in the natural sense. The small crowd meant that we had been rejected by the people of San Pedro Sula. They did not believe what we had been telling them for weeks now. They did not believe Jesus would save them and heal their minds and bodies.

For a few seconds as I stood looking out over the crowd of church people, "Old Slewfoot" attempted to discourage me by saying, "I told you so! These people will not believe you, and you are going to be the laughing stock of the city." But it was like pouring water on a duck's back. None of it soaked in.

In reply to the Devil's lies, I jumped straight up and shouted as loudly as I could, "Hallelujah!" It was so sudden and so loud that the people jumped. I shouted again and again. Presently, the people caught on and began shouting back at me.

As we shouted praises to God, the Spirit of the Lord began moving among the people. A heavy anointing rested over the crowd and over the platform. I began telling them about the love of Jesus and how He died for their sins. The words shot out of my mouth like machine gun bullets. It seemed that every word was dealing a mortal blow to some demonic spirit lurking in the area. When I gave the invitation to accept Christ, several hundred people ran to the front and knelt around the platform. They began calling on God to forgive them of their sins.

I knew there were not many in this crowd who needed miracle healing, but I began praying for the sick *en masse*, calling out different ailments as I prayed. I then asked for those who felt they were healed to come forward and talk with one of our team members. If their healing could be verified, they were asked to come to the platform and testify over the loudspeakers.

A good many people received healing that night and several growths disappeared. I then asked the people to turn and face the city, to stretch out their hands and pray for God's deliverance of San Pedro Sula.

The next night the crowd had grown to about 1,500. Word was getting around. Then on the third night, God began performing mighty miracles. Several cripples — people who were known by those in the city — were instantly healed.

From that night on, the crowds began to grow until we were preaching to 20,000 people each night. On the last few nights the crowds grew to over 25,000. Thousands were responding each evening to the call for salvation.

We had no chairs except those on the platform and a few right down in front for the team members and counselors. The people had to either stand or sit on the ground throughout the meetings, which sometimes lasted for several hours. When the crowds grew, the people crowded together to get nearer the front. Even if they had wanted to sit down, there was usually not enough room. The field turned to thick dust and we had to hire water trucks to wet it down during the day. But despite these problems, God was moving and the miracles began to flow.

One afternoon we were asked to go to the television station to talk about our meeting. When I walked out of the production room, the halls were jammed with crowds of people. They had seen us on television and had rushed to the station for prayer. We were there for over two hours praying for the crowds of sick people. We worked our way down the hall and out the front door while laying hands on the people and praying for their healing.

God began granting outstanding miracles in the meetings. Sometimes while I was still preaching, even before I began praying for the sick, God's miracle power moved through the crowds, healing people. I could tell when the miracles were taking place because little excited crowds gathered here and there throughout the audience as the people moved in close around those being healed. Sometimes people would throw their canes, crutches, or walking sticks toward the platform as they received their healing.

People would then push their way toward the front, praising God for their healing. It became impossible for us to keep up with all the miraculous healings. Many blind eyes were opened. Sometimes the sick who had come in wheelchairs walked away, pushing their wheelchairs ahead of them. Most of the poor unfortunate cripples, who could not afford wheelchairs, were pulled in wagons or on some sort of homemade contrivance. It was interesting to see the unusual ways people had improvised to aid in walking.

The Miracle of Kiki Ponting

One of the most outstanding miracles of the San Pedro Sula crusade was the salvation and healing of Kiki Ponting, the city's political leader and one of the most powerful men in Honduras. Kiki Ponting was well known by everyone in the city as a Communist Party leader and was the meanest and most feared man in that part of the nation.

As a strong political leader, Kiki was instrumental in getting the President of Honduras into office. He was wealthy and owned several businesses as well as the banana plantation.

Kiki Ponting was an avowed atheist with no desire for God. He was a man possessed with hate. He hated himself; he hated God; he hated everyone, and he couldn't get along with his family. But he was also a very sick man. He had been to the States several times trying to get help from the American doctors, but none had been able to determine what was wrong with him. Unable to hold anything in his stomach, he was steadily wasting away.

When his wife saw our telecast in which people were testifying to having been healed in our meetings, she urged Kiki to attend. At first he resisted, but everywhere he went in San Pedro Sula he either heard or saw an announcement proclaiming that Jesus Christ loved him and would save and heal him. We had rained thousands of handbills down over the city from our plane; and when Kiki looked up at a street crossing, he saw our huge banner flying in the breeze telling him, "Jesus Saves And Heals."

About the fifth or sixth night, Kiki and his family began coming to the meetings. To secure good seats he sent his servants to set up chairs in the front near the platform long before time for the service to begin. Each night after the service had started, the Pontings strolled to the front of the crowd and took the chairs from the waiting servants. Kiki always had two six-shooters strapped to his hips. Needless to say, the crowd gave him plenty of room.

It was said that he carried the guns because there were so many people out to kill him. The local pastors told us that he had once caught twenty men stealing bananas from his plantation and had held them with a machine gun for a full day in the hot sun with no food or water while they were forced to hoe grass on his land.

On the fourth night that he came to the crusade, something began to happen to Kiki. He had heard the Word of God preached. He had heard hundreds of testimonies of healing. He had witnessed miracles of healing each night. Through all of this, Kiki had been in excruciating pain. Occasionally, he bent over double because of it. Then on the fourth night, while he was sitting on his chair, listening to the Word of God, his pain suddenly left.

Kiki stood up and grabbed his wife. "I have no more pain!" he shouted. "The pain is gone! Something has happened to me! Something wonderful!"

That night Ponting and his whole family answered the invitation for salvation. A few nights later, they all received the baptism of the Holy Spirit. Kiki was ecstatic with the joy of the Lord. He came to the platform and held the crowd spellbound while he gave his testimony. Everyone knew him and what he had been. When he talked, the people of San Pedro Sula listened.

Kiki commanded one of the team members to accompany him in the daytime as he went from one businessman to another, giving his testimony of how Jesus had saved him, healed him, and baptized him in the Holy Spirit. Hardened, ruthless businessmen fell to their knees and cried like babies when Kiki gave his testimony and witnessed to them about the love of God in sending His Son Jesus to die for them. Kiki went to all the political leaders he had helped put in office and gave them his testimony. He began by saying, "Look, you know, we drank together; we chased women together. But now I am different.

Jesus Christ has come into my life and has made me a different person, a new man."

Kiki always broke down and cried while giving his testimony. He gave his testimony on television and cried like a newborn babe through most of the program. He said, "Once I was on political platforms, but now I am on a platform for Jesus Christ." His testimony, carried on television stations all over Honduras, shook the whole country. The people knew there had to be something to Kiki's new faith, something dynamic, to cause him to change so completely.

Eventually Kiki Ponting went into full-time ministry and helped establish many churches in Honduras. He has visited me in the States and given his testimony here as well.

The Miracle of "Sachmo"

We had begun referring to the old black man with the trumpet as "Sachmo," because of his resemblance to Louis Armstrong. It was a while before the old man would come to any of the meetings; but finally one evening before services began, old Sachmo came dragging onto the field. He could get around, but only with a great deal of effort. His right arm and leg were useless because of the paralysis, but he still managed to walk with a crutch, dragging his right leg. Though he seated himself in one of the chairs near the platform, I did not know he was in the service until near the end.

At the end of the service, the old man was especially attentive to the testimonies of healing. He watched a mother and her young boy, whose crippled hand had been healed, go to the platform and demonstrate what God had done for them. Because the mother and boy had been near Sachmo during the service, the old man had no doubts that the boy's hand had been crippled.

When the old trumpet player saw that formerly paralyzed little boy opening and closing his hand, he said to himself, "If God can heal that little boy, He can heal me." So he stood to his feet and slowly began trying to raise his paralyzed right arm just as he had seen the boy do to demonstrate his miracle. Ever so slowly, he moved his right arm upward. Then, with upraised arm, he moved his hand and fingers. Next, he took steps with his formerly paralyzed right leg.

Suddenly, a great commotion broke out down front near the platform. The old trumpet player was shouting and dancing a jig all around the front of the platform! He could speak plainly; he could move his limbs. God had completely healed him!

Everyone in San Pedro Sula knew him. For years he had played his famous trumpet at every town festival. Then he had become paralyzed by a series of strokes and, as a result, everyone knew him as the town beggar.

When old Sachmo gave his testimony before that crowd of over 20,000 people, they went wild! The team members on the platform hugged one another, clasped hands, and danced a circle around him, singing praises to God. It seemed like hours before the deafening sound of the crowd quietened.

A Boy Delivered From Demons

Another outstanding, and certainly emotionally stirring, miracle was the healing and deliverance of a ten-year-old boy possessed of demons. The lad was so uncontrollable that his parents had kept him chained to a wall. When loose, he would beat his head, bite and kick those around him, and throw himself on the ground in a raging fit. He was worse than a wild animal. All the people at the crusade from his village knew him.

He had broken loose the night before and wandered some forty-five miles to end up in our meeting just when God was performing miracles all through the crowd. We first noticed the boy when he fell on the ground before the platform, screaming. He had gone into a maniacal rage. The power of God was warring against the evil spirits within him, and he went wild. He began kicking and clawing people near him. Then he threw himself back down and beat his head as hard as he could on the ground.

Two of our workers jumped off the platform and grabbed him, but that small boy sent those two grown men rolling in the mud. He was so under the influence of demonic power that it took five men to hold him.

The counselors dragged the boy behind the platform and began ministering to him. While they held him and prayed, I spoke to the demon spirits and commanded them to leave, in Jesus' name. One by one, the evil spirits left the boy.

After he had been delivered and completely set free, he stood on the platform with a big smile on his face. His eyes showed peace and love rather than hatred and fear. He did not look like the same child.

After that, he came to the meetings every night and sat as close as possible to the platform. He would walk up to us, throw his arms around us, and say, "You are my friend. I was *loco* in the *cabeza,* but now I am free." Then he would follow us around before each service started. He was so grateful for what God had done for him.

9
Miracles In The Rain

Blowing sheets of rain hit me head-on as I walked toward the platform. The crusade field, once dry and covered with several inches of powdered dust, was now a lake of mud with puddles of water scattered here and there.

"Let's oil our feathers and make like ducks!" I called out to team members as they attempted to erect a tarpaulin cover over at least one amplifier and loudspeaker for the night meeting. We had left the other equipment wrapped tightly in protective covers.

All of us were huddled under our slickers trying to keep at least partially dry.

Just when I was about to give up on the meeting, several people waded out onto the field with blankets over their heads. Behind them came other groups — men with sombreros pulled down over their eyes, women and children huddled under blankets. More people followed. It seemed as if they had been waiting on the sidelines for the first brave soul to step out.

In a short while the rain slackened, and the field began to fill up around the platform with blanketed forms. When we started the service, there were probably a thousand men, women, and children standing on the wet field in the misty rain. As the men moved their heads, the rainwater ran off the brims of their gigantic roofs.

Had all the people been local folks from San Pedro Sula, it would have been good sense simply to have dismissed the service. However, some of these people had walked for miles from surrounding villages to get to the meeting.

What's a little rain? We won't melt, I thought as I climbed the slippery steps to the platform.

A misty rain was still falling when I started preaching. My heart was drawn to those poor rain-soaked people, many of whom were sick.

I had just plunged into the message when a commotion and stir on the edge of the crowd caught my eye. A woman was crawling to the service. She moved along by dragging her feet and walking on her knees. Her legs and dress were covered with mud. The people made room for her, and she became lost from my view in the crowd.

Later, some of our counselors talked with her and discovered that she had crawled for three and a half miles to be in the service. She had heard about the mighty healing miracles and had come for her healing. She said that she could not wait until it quit raining, but had started for the service that day after learning about the miracles.

God honored the faith and sacrifice of those who had come in the rain and did many miracles that night. His anointing fell over that drenched audience, and people began getting healed right and left.

After the San Pedro Sula Crusade, we moved to Tegucigalpa, the capital city of Honduras. The only place available for our crusade was a dried-up river bed where the river, which flows through the city, had changed its course and had left a small creek in its place.

This river bed was a perfect spot for the crusade because it was right in the middle of the city next to a huge marketplace where about 50,000 people came daily to trade. What we didn't realize when the site was first selected was that it was also used as a toilet area by those 50,000 people who attended the market every day. It was the dung pile of the city!

After making this unpleasant discovery about the field, one of the team members, who had flown down from San Pedro Sula to do some advance work for the crusade, attempted to get a ball park; but the ball park was not available when we needed it. It seemed that our only recourse was to cancel plans for the crusade.

However, the next night as this same team member was praying, the Holy Spirit spoke to him: "Was not Jesus, God's Son, crucified outside the city on a dunghill?" He then called me and we made plans to go on with the crusade. We felt God had spoken and was directing our steps.

As plans advanced for the crusade, God miraculously supplied a road-grading machine to clean the field. One morning when our team was trying to clean the field with shovels and rakes, a man with a road grader drove by. He voluntarily worked on the field for two days without pay.

The field was located between two bridges about a fourth of a mile apart where two highways crossed the river. The field was plowed and graded completely level between the bridges. We then put signs around the field requesting that people use the area under the bridge as a toilet. It was even necessary to post guards during the hours that the market was open.

The local pastors warned us that we would never get the rich people to come to our meeting. But God's miracles draw people from all walks of life.

Even kings were interested in the earthly ministry of Jesus.

Many people had already heard about these outstanding miracles during the San Pedro Sula Crusade, so we started the meeting with a crowd of over 7,000. Attendance grew until one night 35,000 people crowded onto that dunghill to see the miracles of God. There was an average attendance of 20,000.

One afternoon during the middle of the crusade a gully-washer rainstorm came. It poured down for three hours and was still pouring at service time. The workers had already gone ahead to provide for the meeting.

I turned to my interpreter who had been praying with me all afternoon and said, "Adon, we are going to go on with the meeting, but there won't be over five people there besides our workers. The streets are flooding and everyone has headed for shelter by now. In fact, we'll be doing good if we are able to drive in this flood."

I certainly wasn't speaking in faith, but I had no idea how desperately hungry those people were for God. When we drove up, at least 1,000 people were standing in the forceful rain, up to their ankles in mud and water. A few had umbrellas, but most had only blankets or sombreros.

When we drove up to the field, I turned to Adon and said, "Brother, I don't know how you feel, but these people are standing in this flood to hear about Jesus, so I'm going out there and preach."

"Count me with you. I am going, too," Adon said, opening the car door to run for the platform.

The workers had all the equipment covered as well as possible, considering the wind and driving rain. It was difficult to keep the covers tied down.

Several of the fellows held a plastic cover over the microphone while I preached a short sermon to build their faith.

The power of God came down so heavily that I forgot about the wind and pouring rain. The rain never let up that night, but it could have been the Spirit of God raining down on us for all we cared. There were more miraculous healings than we could tally. Since the crowd began leaving immediately after the meeting that night, we did not have a chance to interview the people or have anyone come up to testify as we usually did.

God greatly blessed the Tegucigalpa Crusade. Channel 5 Television came out and filmed thirty minutes of the meeting each night for five nights and captured on film one of the most outstanding miracles of my ministry.

The last night of the crusade, when Channel 5 Television was there filming, a twenty-one-year-old boy, crippled with polio from the time he was ten months old, was completely healed. He had come to the meeting in a wheelchair with braces on his legs. After I had preached under a heavy anointing that night, miracles began happening all over the audience. There were so many instant healings it was impossible for us to keep up with them.

I did not even see the healing of the crippled boy until later when I saw it on television, which proves that I have nothing to do with the miracles. I simply obey God in ministering to the people and allow the gift of miracles to flow through my life when I minister. I am simply a vessel used by God.

Praise God, the television cameraman saw a commotion around the boy in the wheelchair and responded quickly enough to film the complete process of the miracle. The boy got up out of the wheelchair, walked all the way to the front, climbed the ramp, and walked up on the platform. He would not allow anyone to help him.

Many of the people knew that this boy had never walked, so the crowd went wild when that formerly crippled boy walked for the first time in his life. Of course, he was very weak and his walking was slow, but he finally made it to the platform and gave his testimony to the crowd of probably 30,000 people. And because that great miracle was documented on film from beginning to end, millions of people in several nations were able to witness it through television. Only God knows the far-reaching effects of this boy's testimony, and only God could have planned it so well.

In addition to giving us thirty minutes of prime time every day during the crusade, Channel 5 also allowed us to appear on a program at the station. Through our ministry at this station, several employees of Channel 5 were won to the Lord. In fact, real festival broke out at the station. Eventually nearly all the employees were saved and Spirit-filled. All this led up to a miracle that occurred when Channel 5 broadcast a nightly thirty-minute news special filmed at the crusade and shown in several nations.

In our American churches we often pray for God to give us miracles; but in these crusades miraculous healings became so common that we were almost in danger of taking them for granted and forgetting to praise God as we should. Between 500 and 1,000 people came on the platform each night to give their testimony of healing.

Many cripples got up out of wheelchairs or threw aside crutches and walked. A great number of totally blind people were instantly healed. We witnessed hundreds of outstanding miracles every night.

And this same miracle-working power is available to you today, **right now,** there where you are, if you will **exercise your faith to receive it** as these people did in Latin America.

10
You Can Receive Miracles

Since 1955 Dolly and I have been in the ministry and have helped thousands of people receive the miracles they have needed — healing, deliverance, miraculous provision for every kind of need imaginable.

Alcoholics have been instantly delivered and completely set free. Marriages have been saved and restored. Financial problems have been solved. Parent-child relationships have been healed. Creative miracles have replaced organs within bodies. Even the dead have been raised to life on several occasions.

I want to encourage you to believe God for a miracle for your own life as you read this book. I am going to share some testimonies of outstanding miracles that we have witnessed in our ministry because they will build your faith to receive a miracle in your own life. I set my faith in agreement with yours now, in the name of Jesus, for you to receive the miracle that you need so desperately:

"Father, in the name of Jesus, I decree miracles for those in need."

11
The Eugene May Miracle

A few months ago while ministering in Lafayette, Louisiana, I met Rev. Eugene May, Dean of Lafayette Christian Bible College. Rev. May came forward after the service to give me his testimony. Here it is in his own words:

"I am writing this testimony for the sole purpose of telling the world that the God Who worked through the hands of Jesus and His disciples to bring healing and miracles can and will bring healing and miracles to you.

"My mother had severe difficulties in childbirth when I was born; and, as a result of an infection in my intestinal system, I was plagued with an ulcerated stomach until my twenty-third year. At that time, my doctor told me that the only way I could be helped was for my entire stomach to be removed. I consented to the surgery and, in 1967, my stomach was totally removed.

"At the time of the surgery, I weighed 230 pounds, which was too much for my five-foot, ten-inch frame. As an immediate result of the surgery, I lost 90 pounds and spent the next six years attempting to 'hold my own' against weight loss by eating six or seven small meals a day.

"In early 1973, my wife and I received the baptism of the Holy Spirit while pastoring the First Baptist Church in Greensburg, Louisiana. The truth of healing and miracles opened up to me. During the summer of 1973, I attended a convention at Bethany Baptist Church in Baton Rouge, Louisiana, and heard

Brother Burnie Davis minister the Word and pray for the sick. During one particular service, while preaching on the subject, 'Faith Without Works Is Dead,' Brother Davis stopped and said, 'Somebody's getting a miracle — a big miracle — right now.' Suddenly a man spoke up and said, 'It's me, I can talk.' His vocal cords had been severed and he had not been able to speak for seventeen years.

"At that moment the power of God fell upon the audience. People began to receive healing and miracles all over the congregation. I raised my hands to the Lord and said, 'Lord, my stomach.' I immediately felt as if warm oil had been poured over my head and was running down through my body and out my feet. I knew that God had touched me. In a moment of time, He replaced the stomach which surgery had removed. The only difference was that the new one had no imperfections.

"Immediately I began to eat normal meals and gain weight. Strength returned to my body and every infirmity fled. Before I had had the surgery, I could not eat many foods because of their effect upon my stomach. Suddenly I could eat anything I desired, including very spicy food, which I had always enjoyed but had never been able to eat without severe pain.

"Brother Davis spoke the Word of God, and God honored that Word in me as I acted upon it. God is no respecter of persons. (Rom. 2:11.) He is able, willing, and waiting to heal you or give you the miracle you need *if you will simply ask in faith and act upon the Word.*"

12
The Miracle of "Whiskey Bill"

Alcoholism is one of the biggest problems facing our nation and our world. Not only does it destroy the lives of the alcoholics themselves, but it also produces a domino effect that adversely affects the lives of countless others.

Families and employers suffer along with the alcoholic. Society in general also suffers, when you consider the thousands of traffic fatalities each year that are the direct result of drunken driving, and the great waste of talent and productivity on the part of the alcoholic.

But there is good news for the alcoholic: He can be set free by God's miracle power.

"Whiskey Bill" Heiman was an alcoholic for twenty-five years, a hopeless drunk with no desire to live. Then one day he came to one of our crusades, and God instantly delivered him. But "Whiskey Bill" tells his story in his own words much better than I:

"When I was eighteen years old, I was in the U.S. Navy, stationed at Okinawa, in the South Pacific during World War II. The Japs were throwing everything they had at us when our ship LST #808, was hit and sunk by several bombs and a suicide plane on May 18, 1945. Only one officer and a few of us enlisted men survived and were in the water. The fire, the explosions, and the sound of men screaming for help in the middle of the night was bad enough, but sharks attacked us in the water and finished off what the Japs had left. I thought my time had come when something took my arm and started pulling me.

I had been hurt and was bleeding, and my left leg felt like it was blown off at the knee.

"Finally, I found myself on the beach and saw 'Little Joe,' a black man who had pulled me to safety, turn and start out to get another wounded man. But then he disappeared in the middle of the black water. A shark had got him. I just got sick! Many had died that horrible night, but for some unknown reason, my life was saved.

"After that I started drinking and became a drunk at eighteen. Because I would drink so much whiskey, I got the name 'Whiskey Bill' and kept that name for twenty-five years.

"At the same time that my ship sank, many thousands of miles away, my mother was praying for me. It was 2:30 A.M. in Beaumont, Texas, where she was when God spoke to her and gave her a vision of exactly what was happening in the Pacific. She saw me wounded in the water, bleeding, and surrounded by fire. She saw ships sinking and burning and heard men crying for help.

"Since we hadn't been able to tell where we were or anything that was happening, the Naval Intelligence Officers could not believe how my mother in Texas had described the exact scene in every detail when I let them read her letter. Also in her letter she said that God had spoken to her and said, 'Fear not, I have heard your prayers. Your son is wounded, but I will bring him home safely, and he will preach the Gospel one day.'

"When my mother wrote me and told me that I was going to be a preacher one day, I didn't believe it then, nor did I believe it for twenty-five years. I just drank more than ever until my health was ruined. I had two heart attacks, high blood pressure, and bleeding ulcers. The doctor told me I wouldn't live six months. Despite all this, I still drank every day.

"I attempted suicide twice, yet God spared my life both times. Then, on February 19, 1970, I took an overdose of sleeping pills and drank a fifth of 101-proof whiskey. I sat alone in a night club waiting for my heart to quit beating so that I could die and not hurt anyone again.

"A small girl, whom I had never seen before, came to the juke box which was near my table, selected a song, then disappeared. The song was 'Just a Closer Walk with Thee.' I began to cry and said, 'Jesus, why can't I walk with Thee?' He answered and said, 'You can, Bill, but you must leave this place now!'

"I was so scared that I ran out and went home. After all the sleeping pills and whiskey, I was not one bit sleepy, nor was I dying. Since I couldn't sleep, I got up and went to the barn where I always kept a fifth of whiskey hidden in the feed barrel.

"God spoke to me in a loud, earth-shaking voice and said, 'Don't drink a drop!' I ran outside but saw no one. By this time I was really scared, so I got my bottle the second time. Again in a loud voice God spoke, 'Don't drink a drop!'

"I went into the house to get a cup of coffee. Still shaking, I opened the newspaper. It was Saturday, February 20, 1970, and I saw a large ad saying, 'Do you need deliverance from alcohol? Come to the Burnie Davis Crusade, Holiday Inn, Beaumont, Texas, at 10:00 A.M.'

"I got dressed and arrived there at 9:45 A.M. But when I walked into the large room in the Holiday Inn where the meeting was to be held, I started to cry and beg God to please let me die. I couldn't take it anymore; I'd rather die and go to hell than to hurt my dear wife, my four precious children, and the rest of my family anymore.

"Then Burnie Davis and two other preachers came in. Brother Davis ended the meeting by praying for me, a dying drunk who was broke and had the DT's. Praise God, I didn't know what Brother Davis was saying. I couldn't understand one word because it wasn't English, but I really didn't care how he prayed. If he couldn't reach God, I knew I was dead.

"Then I began to feel like I was standing in something. It felt like warm milk and honey. It began to come up my legs, into my body, and make my heart begin to burn like it was on fire. Then it went out through the top of my head, and I began to cry and laugh. I had never felt healthier and happier in my life. I felt like I was dreaming and in heaven.

"When Brother Davis laid hands on me and prayed, I was saved, completely healed, and filled with the Holy Spirit. Then Brother Davis startled me, an old drunk, by prophesying that I would preach the Gospel in the United States and in foreign lands.

"I went home and tried to tell my precious wife what had happened. I thought she would be happy to hear the good news, but instead she acted like I was drunk. That night I took her and eight other people to Burnie Davis' crusade because I wanted them to get what Jesus had given me.

"Brother Davis prayed for my wife while I was standing behind her. The power of God went through her and almost knocked me off my feet. From that day, she became on fire for Jesus, and has stayed on fire for ten years now. Our lives and marriage become sweeter every day.

"I praise God for forgiving that old, no-good, dying drunk known as 'Whiskey Bill,' for healing me, for filling me with the Holy Spirit, and for calling me to preach the Gospel. Thank You, Jesus!

"For ten years God has blessed us. Now we are pastoring a church, the Christian Center, in Beaumont, Texas. We have just returned from the West Indies and are helping five churches and missions in Trinidad, India, Africa, Colombia (South America), and Mexico.

"Praise God, all that Brother Davis prophesied to me has come to pass. God has given me a completely new life in Jesus Christ."

13
The Opal Smith Miracle

On Sunday night, December 5, 1971, in Montclair, California, I experienced one of the most outstanding miracles of my ministry. Opal Smith came to our crusade a dying woman. She did not come expecting to be healed; she came expecting to die. She came because she was invited by her daughter.

Opal had suffered through twenty-seven operations, and for thirty-two months prior to coming to our meetings, she had been in a coma. Opal tells her own story:

"Most of my past life has been full of pain and sorrow. Before God healed me, I could not remember a day without pain.

"After my husband's death in 1969, I suffered a complete mental and physical breakdown. When I began vomiting blood, the doctors ran tests. At first they said the vomiting was caused by my nerves, but X rays showed I had a bleeding hernia. The only solution was surgery. Because I had diabetes and had undergone so many operations, my flesh was held together by steel mesh. An incision would not heal; therefore, surgery was impossible.

"The bleeding was continuous; sometimes blood filled my throat at night so that I choked. I was rushed to the emergency room several times a week when my stomach became filled with blood from the hemorrhaging.

"Prior to this, in April 1967, I had suffered a severe heart attack, which had left me with a heart condition called angina that caused severe chest pains and an enlarged heart. Of course, this condition made it difficult for me to breath. I also had hardening of the arteries and high blood pressure, which caused a loud throbbing sound in my ears.

"Due to my weakened condition, I fell, breaking my hip, knee, leg, and ankle, and injuring my back. I underwent surgery to set the bones and to insert plastic tubes.

"During surgery, my lung collapsed. The doctors debated about taking off my leg because they were afraid it would never heal due to the diabetes. My leg and foot were twice their normal size. In addition, cancer cells had developed in my body.

"After years of suffering, it looked like the end had finally come in October of 1971. I was rushed to the Pomona Valley Hospital emergency room and, while there, was examined by a neurologist to determine if there was any way to alleviate my terrible pain. After a thorough examination, the doctor told me that there was nothing medical science could do for me.

"The neurologist said that no medicine could help me for I was dying. His words hit my mind and heart with the force of the blow of a sledgehammer. For me, there was no hope. The doctor loaded me down with medicine to ease the pain and sent me home to die.

"My daughter, Sue, stopped by my house on Saturday afternoon, December 4, 1971, to tell me about an ad she had seen in the paper for a miracle healing service. I was a Christian and believed in prayer for the sick; however, I had been prayed for so many times in my life that I had decided to give up completely. I wanted no more doctors and no more prayers.

"My daughter went to the Burnie Davis Miracle Crusade on Sunday morning, December 5, and stopped by that afternoon to tell me of the miracles she had seen. I became excited and attended the meeting with her that night, not because I thought about being healed myself, but because I wanted to see the miracles. I had already resigned myself to accepting death. I had completely given up hope.

"During the service, Brother Davis called for someone with a hernia to come forward for healing. He then called for someone with a heart condition. Immediately thereafter he called for someone with a throbbing in their ears. At this point, I began to feel a tingling sensation in my spine. **The thought then flashed before me that God was going to heal me.** I had every symptom that Brother Davis had announced, but it had not dawned on me until that instant that he was talking about me.

"When Brother Davis called for those who needed healing to come forward, I walked to the front. Brother Davis called me out of the healing line to be prayed for first. When he asked about my condition, I told him about the throbbing in my ears and that I was sick all over. He laid his hands on my head and prayed, 'Lord, I cannot do this, but You can.'

"He then had me sit on a chair so he could measure the length of my leg. When he lifted my legs, the pain was so great that I slid down in the chair to release the pressure on my spine. One leg was shorter than the other and my ankle was still swollen to twice its normal size. When Brother Davis prayed, the ankle returned to normal size almost immediately, and one leg grew out to the same length of the other.

"Then Brother Davis asked me to stand up, bend over, and touch the floor. I knew that if I could do that, something had happened, for the doctors had told me that as long as the steel mesh was in my stomach and the eight-inch steel rod was in my back, I would never be able to bend over.

"Brother Davis commanded me, in the name of Jesus, to bend over and touch the floor. And that is exactly what I did, with absolutely no pain whatever! That meant something had happened to that steel mesh which was attached to both hips and pulled across my stomach to hold my insides together! And something had happened to the eight inches of steel in my back!

"The throbbing had left my ears. All pain was gone. For the first time since breaking my leg in 1967, I was able to put all my weight on that leg. All the swelling was gone. I could breathe deeply again without pain. **I pushed my hand into my stomach, but I could not detect the steel screen.**

"I dropped my glasses and broke them later on December 15, 1971. I had always had a lot of problems with my eyes and had been told that I would need eye surgery. But when I went in for an examination, I was told that I needed no surgery because my eyes were perfect.

"In January of 1972, I went to the San Bernardino County Hospital in San Bernardino, California, for a complete examination and tests. The X rays showed no metal in my body. The sugar tests showed no sugar in my blood. There was no evidence of bleeding in my stomach. My heart and blood pressure were normal. And there was no evidence of cancer in my body!

"I was then examined again by my personal doctor, who could find nothing wrong with me. He wanted to know what had happened to me, and I was able to testify to him about the healing power of the Lord Jesus Christ.

"I shall always praise God for healings and miracles and for my complete deliverance from the bondage Satan had put upon me."

* * * * *

If God could heal Opal Smith, He can certainly heal you, no matter what your condition might be. In the name of Jesus, I set my faith in agreement with you right now for a complete and total healing. I am believing with you now, as you read this, for God's miracle power to reach you and touch you.

Receive it, in the name of Jesus!

14
How You Can Activate The Working of Miracles

Up to this point everything in this book has simply been an introduction to what we are going to discuss from here on. I believe this is without a doubt the most important message you will ever receive, outside of the message that led you to accept Jesus Christ as your personal Savior.

Why do I make this bold statement? Because reaching the unreached with the gospel message is the very heartthrob of the Lord Jesus. In Mark 16:15, just before He was taken up to be with the Father, Jesus said to His disciples: *Go ye into all the world, and preach the gospel to every creature.* He went on to say that every believer could have a ministry with signs following (Mark 16:17,18) — in other words, a miracle ministry.

Why is it so important to have a miracle ministry? Because miracles are the very theme of the Bible, from the miracle creation of the universe and of man, to the prophecy of the miracle return of the Lord Jesus.

Miracles are a sign to the unbeliever — a sign of God's existence and of His supernatural power. Jesus gave to the unbelieving the sign of His miracles to show forth His deity. Jesus has commanded us to do the same. Miracles are God's sign to the unbeliever.

Jesus performed miracles. The apostles performed miracles throughout the book of Acts.

Nearly one-half of the world's 4.3 billion people have not yet heard about Jesus Christ. I ask you: Do they not have the right to witness God's sign, His miracle power, so that they might believe upon the Lord Jesus Christ and be saved?

The responsibility of demonstrating God's miracle power to the unbeliever rests upon every believer. Not only is a miracle ministry our right, it is also our responsibility.

Notice in the eighth chapter of the book of Acts the pattern for reaching the unreached with the gospel message. First, the Word is preached. Second, God confirms His Word among the unreached by the working of miracles. Third, because of the miracles which the unbeliever both sees and hears, he accepts Christ as his Savior.

To most Christians, a miracle ministry is a great mystery, something only a few ministers are ever blessed with. The miracle ministry has been shrouded with great mystery. These ministries have stood a notch or two above the others so that we could never get close to them to find out how they work. Consequently, few have ever moved into the working of miracles.

But, praise God, I have been able to teach many others how to activate the working of miracles in their own ministries. I do this by sharing with them (as I have with you in this book) my own personal experience in this area so that they will say (as I hope you will also), "Bless God, if Burnie Davis can do those miracles through the name of Jesus, I can do them too!"

I also share with them some biblical principles concerning the working of miracles. Let us now examine together some of these scriptures:

First Corinthians 12:10 — . . . *to another the working of miracles.* Verse 29 of that chapter refers to *workers of miracles.*

John 14:12 — *Verily, verily, I say unto you, He that believeth on me, the works that I* (Jesus) *do shall he do also; and greater works than these shall he do; because I go unto my Father.* Notice the words *working, workers, you, he,* and *shall he do.*

Peter said to the lame man in Acts 3:6, . . . *such as I have give I thee: In the name of Jesus Christ of Nazareth rise up and walk.* And he did!

How did Peter work that miracle?

First you have to believe that you have received something before you can give it. Peter believed the words Jesus spoke to His disciples in John 14:12 (above) and in Acts 1:8: *Ye shall receive power, after that the Holy Ghost is come upon you . . . .* Also in Mark 16:17,18 He said, *And these signs shall follow them that believe; In my name shall they cast out devils; they shall . . . lay hands on the sick, and they shall recover.*

Consequently, with ease and authority Peter said to that crippled beggar, "I give you what I have" — which was the power of the Spirit, the God-working part of the miracle. (1 Cor. 12:11.)

The miracle-working Spirit was given *in the name of Jesus* as Peter said, *Rise up and walk.* Then his faith (action) went further when he took the lame man by the hand and lifted him up.

Now look at Mark 16:20: *And they went forth, and preached every where* (that's what **they** did), *the Lord working with them, and confirming the word* (that's what **God** did) *with signs following.*

When Peter gave the spirit of the working of miracles **by his words,** in the name of Jesus, then took the cripple by the hand, lifting (or touching, or laying on of hands), then God worked within him (God had something to work with). **It was the Word of God that God confirmed.**

Now, notice in 1 Corinthians 12:4-11 every place (and how many times) it says *the same Spirit* or *the selfsame Spirit*, and how He divided *to every man severally as he will.*

The *same Spirit* we yield to and act on to prophesy or to speak in tongues or discern spirits is the exact *same Spirit* (not another) that we yield to and act on to work miracles. It is no harder to work miracles than to speak in tongues or to prophesy.

Probably the difference is in environment. If you have been in an environment where there is much prophesying, that's what you understand and believe you can do.

I was brought up in an environment not only of prophesying, but of miracles and healings. Consequently, it is easy for me to expect and take action for miracles. Jesus said, *According to your faith be it unto you* (Matt. 9:29).

When Opal Smith stood in front of me in Montclair, California, a few years ago, it was not difficult at all to witness her miracle take place right before our eyes.

The swelling in her leg went down and her ankle became free instantly. The left leg grew out three fourths of an inch. The pounding in her ears stopped. I had her bend over and touch the floor, which in the natural she could not do. But with the Holy Spirit — the One Who, working with us, puts into gear the working of miracles — it was simple.

After two months of examination, Opal Smith was given a clean bill of health by the same doctors and hospital who had worked with her for years. The steel-screen plate and the eight-inch rod were gone.

Even the plastic parts that had replaced some organs had turned to flesh. She had a new backbone, and they described her nerves as "looking like a baby's."

The other night as I laid my hands on a man whose eardrum had been removed, leaving him stone deaf in that left ear, I could feel the Holy Spirit in me shift into gear — the gift of the working of miracles in cooperation with my working of faith (acting on what God said). **God will work with you, not without you!** (Mark 16:20.) Instantly the man could hear even a whisper.

You can stir up the gifts by sharing the scriptures on the subject first, through teaching and preaching.

Seek the *best gift* (1 Cor. 12:31) for the situation and need. You can be God's hand extended, reaching out to the oppressed of the world. With confidence in supernatural help, we can go *into all the world, and preach the gospel to every creature.*

The same principle applies to giving. When you give, you activate the Spirit of God to confirm what He said He would do — which is to give back to you *good measure, pressed down, and shaken together, and running over* (Luke 6:38). When you give, God causes men to give unto you.

God will work **with you** and confirm His Word with signs following when you **act on** His Word!

15
The Working of Miracles

Jesus was *approved of God . . . by miracles and wonders and signs, which God did by him . . .* (Acts 2:22).

God the Father did the miracles, signs, and wonders by (via) Jesus. Jesus said that He didn't do anything but what the Father showed Him first. (John 8:28,29; 14:10.) He said He came to show us the Father plainly. He said, "If you have seen Me, you have seen the Father." (John 14:9.) In other words, He was saying, "The works that I do is the Father working in Me and through Me." (John 14:11.) God *is* the Miracle Worker.

It is also right to say that Jesus is a miracle worker because He certainly had His part, too. But it was God Who anointed Him with the Holy Ghost, giving him the power to do it. The Father had a job for Him to do, and as long as He was "about His Father's business," when He needed a miracle, He got it — just in the normal course of doing God's will. **Folks, this is the great secret! Be doers and not hearers only.** (James 1:22.) **Faith without works is dead!** (James 2:26.)

How did Jesus perform miracles? First, He knew that God was with Him. He was in constant fellowship with the Father.

How did He turn the water into wine? (John 2:1-10.) When you are in constant fellowship with the Miracle Worker, it is easy! All He did was say, "Fill the water pots full of water and go pour it in the drinking vessels." Nothing to it! Ah, but there was more. There was God, Who is a Spirit, working *with* Him in whatever He did.

Jesus wanted to bless Peter for letting Him use his boat to preach from. (Luke 5:1-7.) He simply said, "Launch out and let down your nets on the other side." That's all. As Peter obeyed Jesus, going against his own knowledge of fishing, the miracle came to pass — the nets were filled to overflowing.

In both miracles you see that *faith action* was required on the part of the ones He spoke to. God will work **with you** to confirm His Word. In the normal course of His ministry, Jesus needed miracles. **Any one who is out doing something for God will need miracles all the time.**

Jesus finished teaching, but the people still followed Him. The disciples said, "Send them away." But Jesus said, "Feed them." The disciples were quick to tell Him there was no food, but a little boy came up with one little lunch. Just one. That's all. Enough for one little boy.

Believing in miracles, Jesus said, "Bring the lunch," and blessed it. In the act of breaking it, there came the miracle of multiplication, and it fed 5,000 men, plus many women and children. They all ate their fill, and there was plenty left over. (John 6:1-14.)

Tax time came and there wasn't money to pay the taxes. But Jesus had been about His Father's business, doing what His Father showed Him to do. When a miracle was needed, there was nothing to it!

You don't have to go around looking for a need for a miracle — needs will just arise because we live in a world that is opposed to the will of God. Certainly the Devil will oppose! And, too, sometimes the work of God cuts right across the natural, so you need a miracle.

When Jesus needed tax money, He sent Peter fishing. And the first fish Peter caught had enough money in its mouth to pay the taxes. (Matt. 17:24-27.)

Jesus needed to go to His disciples when they were out in their boat, so He just walked on the water. (Matt. 14:25.) Would you agree that that was a miracle?

Recently, in the course of our working for and with God, the need for a miracle arose. It was in the form of a land payment of $16,500 which was due within three weeks, nonrenewable. I went to prayer, and the Holy Spirit spoke to me to send three letters — no more, no less. The first to inform my friends of the need — the next two, updates of the first.

I obeyed the Holy Spirit. I acted my faith. The rest was up to God who said that men would give. (Luke 6:38.) I was almost amazed when so many responded. I knew God was working with us to confirm His Word, because normally we just don't get that much.

First Corinthians 12:11 says that all nine of the gifts are of the *selfsame Spirit,* including the *working of miracles.* Notice that they are gifts of the (Holy) Spirit, not gifts of men. They operate only as He (the Holy Spirit) wills, not as man wills.

How do we activate the Holy Spirit to manifest the gifts or gift we need at the moment? Since we are talking specifically about *working of miracles,* let's zero in on some examples of how to activate the working of miracles on our behalf.

All through the Word of God, you will see that great miracles were brought about by men who **acted upon** God's Word.

Let me re-emphasize that the gifts mentioned in the twelfth chapter of First Corinthians are the tools that the Holy Spirit uses to confirm the Word on which we are acting. The Word says, *Quench not the Spirit* (1 Thess. 5:19), and, *Grieve not the holy Spirit of God* (Eph. 4:30). The Word also says to *stir up the gift . . . which is in thee* (2 Tim. 1:6). That gift is the Holy Spirit. **If you stir Him up and give Him liberty, then you will see signs and wonders.** If you please the Father, then you please the Holy Spirit, because they work together. (1 Cor. 12:4-6.)

Faith, trust, and *utter dependence* on God's Word will please God. The Father responded to the *need* of mankind when He gave His only begotten Son, Jesus. But He doesn't respond to needs anymore; He responds to **faith. Faith** is the victory. (1 John 5:4.) Hebrews 11:6 says, *Without faith it is impossible . . . . According to your faith be it unto you,* Jesus said in Matthew 9:29.

You can activate the Holy spirit in you by putting your faith in action. The Holy Spirit in you will get excited when you show that you trust the Word of the Father. The Word and the Spirit agree. In fact, the Word we read in the Bible was written down by men who were inspired by the Holy Spirit.

In Joshua 6:2-5,16, God told Joshua that He had given him the city of Jericho. But this didn't mean that Joshua and the children of Israel were to sit and wait until it happened automatically. *They had to do something.* God told them what to do to possess the land that He had already given them. They had to believe enough to act. When they acted their faith; the miracle, the supernatural cooperation, came; and **the walls fell down.** (v. 20.)

Many people have passive faith instead of active faith. They are waiting for something to come their way, but they are not the ones who get miracles!

In Luke 5:18-25 four men brought a palsied man to the house where Jesus was teaching, where *the power of the Lord was present to heal . . .* (v. 17). Verse 20 says, *And when he saw their faith, he said unto him, Man, thy sins are forgiven thee.* And in verse 24, *Arise, and take up thy couch, and go into thine house.* Verse 25 says the man did it without argument or hesitation.

Don't just act on the Word — or what you believe to be God speaking to you — in a dry fashion, or just because you saw or heard how someone else did it. Pray and meditate on the scriptures that pertain to your situation until the Spirit of Truth gets into your spirit and becomes a part of you, so that you know that what you are about to do is right. When that truth occupies your thoughts and brings you joy and peace, get after it, because that's faith, and the Lord is going to work with you to confirm His Word with signs following! (Mark 16:20.)

It's just like playing a game of checkers. You move; God moves. He is a perfect gentleman; He never moves out of turn. He is patient — He will sit and wait with you. Or He will get up and move with you. When you get into action, He will get into action, too, to confirm the Word you are acting on.

God has promised to bless everything you put your hands to, so put your hands to something!

16
How To Move Into A Miracle Ministry

I have had people tell me that it would not be possible to work miracles in some particular church because of the unbelief of the people there. Then they would swell out their chests and proudly point out how Mark 6:5,6 states that even Jesus could not do any mighty miracles in Nazareth *because of their unbelief.*

But I want you to know right now that whenever Jesus found one person in a crowd, just one with a big enough need to cause him to reach out in faith toward Him, Jesus overroad the unbelief of the others and performed a miracle for that one.

The twelfth chapter of Matthew describes the day Jesus was ministering in a crowd full of unbelief. A man with a withered hand had a need, a desperate need, and he also had faith. Did Jesus let the unbelief of that crowd prevent Him from performing the miracle? No! He propelled the miracle-healing power of God right out of His Spirit toward that one in need of a miracle. The unbelief of the crowd could not hold back the miracle power of God!

You can perceive the spirit of unbelief in a crowd; but you can also overpower it, just as Jesus did. If you do not learn that, then you will not receive many miracles in your ministry.

When Jesus was in that crowd of unbelieving people in Nazareth, He *could there do no mighty work, save that he laid his hands upon a few sick folk, and healed them* (Mark 6:5). It was not a case of His laying His hands on people's heads and their not getting healed. They were healed when He laid His hands on them — all of them. The problem was that because of their unbelief, only *a few* would step out of the crowd and come to Him for prayer. But those who did come to Him received their miracle — just as surely as those in believing crowds.

When you stand before a crowd of unbelieving witch doctors in a heathen land, you stand as the anointed of God, just as Jesus was the anointed Christ. That same miracle power that was in Jesus is in you.

The miracle power is in you! It is in you, but it won't do any good in you. **You must get it out of you and onto the sick and dying unbelievers who stand before you.**

Suppose you have stood on a crude platform and said the words of God. And the dark, dirty, sweaty faces staring at you have heard the words that proceeded forth from your mouth and are now patiently waiting for the miracles you have told them about.

What will you do now?

Will you yield to unbelief and allow it to lock up the miracle power inside you?

Will you deny them the right to know there is a miracle-working God?

No! You will not yield to unbelief. You will activate the mighty miracle-working power of God by believing it right out of you and onto the people who are standing before you. *You believe the miracle power right out of your spirit and onto them for the miracle they need!*

When you have learned to do this, you have learned how to activate the working of miracles!

My youngest brother Rick learned to move into a miracle ministry while working with me on a crusade. I was behind the platform prayng while the music and singing were being conducted. Rick was seated on the platform with a great number of missionaries and National preachers.

Suddenly, Rick came running up to me, shouting, "Burnie, come quickly! A woman has died. What shall I do?"

I turned and looked straight at Rick. "Well, we have announced miracles to the people for this crusade. Go raise her up, in the name of Jesus."

Rick stammered and stuttered in fright for a few seconds. When I insisted, he went out and raised up that woman, in the name of Jesus. Rick learned in front of thousands of people and a group of denominational missionaries that the responsibility for miracles was up to God, not him. He simply applied the Word of God. God always backs His Word with signs following when that Word goes forth in faith.

You see, it is not automatic as we once supposed it to be. And God does not just start performing miracles without our knowledge of it. These gifts all come by the same Spirit. It is no more difficult to believe for the working of miracles than it is to have faith in prophesy or to speak in other tongues. These gifts all work by the same Spirit.

When I first began ministering God's miracle power, I nearly always laid my hands upon the sick. I believed the miracle power right out of me and through my hands into the people. I could actually feel the tangible power of God when it left my hands and went into the sick.

Then, during a crusade in Brazil, I found myself praying for so many people that my body was exhausted as I was praying into the early hours of the morning. It was then that I learned that I could pray for the audience *en masse.* I could stretch my hands out toward the thousands of sick and believe God's miracle power right out of me and onto them just as I had believed the power out of me and onto the individual.

In praying *en masse* in this way, I have seen hundreds of people healed, all at the same time. This is the way we were praying for the people in the crusades described earlier in this book.

Once when I was ministering in India with Morris Cerullo, I learned something about believing the miracle power of God out and onto the people. Brother Cerullo asked me to accompany him in laying hands on some National ministers and praying for them.

I followed Brother Cerullo as he prayed for the ministers. I laid my hands on them and said a prayer; but I was tired and weary from ministering, so I didn't put much effort into it.

Brother Cerullo turned and shouted at me, "Burnie! Give them something, man! Give them something!"

Yes, Brother Cerullo knew that you have something inside you. Every believer has it. But it doesn't come out automatically. **You have to believe it out of you and onto the people.** You must minister in faith.

17
Ways To Release The Miracle Power

Whether you think it or say it, you release the miracle power of God in the name of Jesus. There are various ways or methods of releasing the power of God. We are perhaps most familiar with the ministry of the **laying on of hands.**

It is possible to lay hands on people and see nothing happen; I have done so. The fault was not God's. I had the miracle-working power of God within me, but I had to believe it out of me. Just as all of the ministering gifts work by faith, so does the working of miracles.

But I also learned that I can minister the working of miracles by **the spoken word.** I can speak God's miracle-healing power right out over an audience and believe God for blind eyes to be opened, for the deaf to hear, for the cripples to walk, for tumors and growths to disappear. I can do it, and I have done it many times.

What am I trying to say here? I want you to understand that the working of miracles is not automatic. **You have to activate the working of the miracles.**

You can stand like a dummy in front of people all day long and lay your hands on their heads until all the hair is rubbed off; but until you activate the working of miracles by releasing your faith, nothing will happen.

You can activate the working of miracles **by telling someone to do something.** Peter and John told the cripple at the Gate Beautiful to arise and walk, in the name of Jesus. (Acts 3:6.)

Or you may activate the working of miracles **by doing something yourself.** Jesus once took clay and rubbed it onto the eyes of a blind man. I remember straightening a hunchback by grabbing him by the shoulders and pulling him up. But I was led by the Holy Spirit to do so.

You can activate the miracle-working power of God in different areas of your life. I have believed God for a miracle to keep a plane flying when it was aerodynamically impossible to remain airborne. I have believed God for life to return to my dead baby when she was killed in an automobile accident; and God performed a miracle and restored her life. I have believed God for miracles when my car was broken down on the highway miles from nowhere, and God performed creative miracles and replaced defective parts.

And with God working in you, you can do the same.

18

How Can You Get Started In The Ministry?

This is a question I am often asked especially by young people, who, in launching out by faith into a new ministry, often have difficulty finding open doors for preaching.

The only way any of us is ever going to get started in the ministry is to **take the first step.** We must act in faith and simply begin ministering.

I remember years ago when I was trying to get started in the ministry. I was married with a new baby and was living with Dad and helping in his church. I was walking the floor, praying, and wondering why no one would ask me to preach in their church.

I even got to the point of grumbling and complaining because God wouldn't open doors for me. Have you ever been there? Some of you have, I know.

One day while I was walking the church floor, praying and reading the Word, the *go ye,* as in *Go ye into all the world, and preach the gospel to every creature* (Mark 16:15) jumped out at me and set off buzzers down in the depths of my spirit. It was like a green light flashing on. **Go!** What you do on a green light is go.

So, I told my wife I was going to preach. When she asked, "Where?" I said, "I don't know." I just climbed into my car and began driving across the country. I came to a town I recognized and remembered a friend who lived there. When I pulled into his driveway, he walked up to the car.

"Burnie, you old rascal!" he said. "God sent you up here."

I said, "He did?"

"Sure," he said, "I have been praying that God would send someone to hold a revival, and here you are!"

And there I was! The miracle power of God had been activated and launched me into the ministry. I was praying that God would open doors, but I wanted God to do it all. I was not willing to step out into the realm of faith and activate the working of miracles.

I remember still another time in my life when I was sidetracked and my preaching ministry had slowed down. I was reading the Word and praying, but I was not out preaching. Dolly and I felt drawn to the mission field, but we were very young and didn't have much money.

Dolly said, "Let's go to Mexico."

It sounded good to me. I just wanted to get away for a while. I was full of unrest as I had not preached for some time.

When we both agreed and made the decision to go to Mexico, someone came to us and offered to pay our expenses. Praise God for miracles!

We headed for a missions convention in Monterrey, Mexico. I did not really expect to preach; I just felt a strong impression in my spirit to go. But when I arrived, Roy Stockstell said to me, "Burnie, I want you to preach in my place tonight."

The next night Ken Sumrall said to me, "The Holy Spirit wants you to preach in my place tonight, Burnie." During that meeting I preached five times. The power of God came down each night. Over 1,000 people were saved and nearly 500 people received the baptism of the Holy Spirit. And none of it was planned by me. Of course, God knew all about it.

I remember a lady coming up to Dolly and me in church before we left for the trip and giving us a prophecy. That was before we knew for sure that we were going. But the lady said that if we went on the trip we were planning, 1,000 people would be saved.

Yes, you can activate the working of miracles to get started in the ministry. But you have **to do something.** You move, and God moves; but God is always a jump ahead of you, preparing the way.

19
Signs and Wonders Follow Those Who Go . . .

And they went forth, and preached every where, the Lord working with them, and confirming the word with signs following.

Mark 16:20

This was confirmation of what Jesus had predicted would happen in Mark 16:15-18. "Go into all the world, preach the Gospel, and these signs shall *follow.*"

If you don't ever go anywhere or do anything, then don't expect any signs and wonders in your ministry — they only *follow.*

Look at Jesus, our example. In Matthew 4:23-25 we read: *And Jesus went about . . . teaching . . . and preaching . . . .* And what happened? *His fame went throughout all Syria: and they brought unto him all sick people that were taken with divers diseases and torments, and those which were possessed with devils, and those which were lunatic, and those that had the palsy; and he healed them.*

And there followed him great multitudes . . . .

No one likes to preach to an empty church or crusade ground. Those who believe in signs and wonders, and who practice them, will have a full church and crusade ground. Those who set Jesus as their example for ministry will go, teach, preach, and heal the sick — and it will work!

Just resist fear, and start. Be a doer of the Word and not a hearer only. James 2:14 says, *What doth it profit, my brethren, though a man say he hath faith, and have not works? Can faith save him?* And verse

17 declares, *Even so faith, if it hath not works, is dead, being alone.* Faith is made perfect in going, saying, doing. (v. 22.)

In Matthew 8:1-3 we read: *When he* (Jesus) *was come down from the mountain, great multitudes followed him. And, behold, there came a leper . . . And Jesus put forth his hand, and touched him . . . and immediately his leprosy was cleansed.*

Notice: Everywhere Jesus *went,* signs and wonders *followed.*

Praise the Lord, that can happen for you, because as He is, so are we. Jesus never intended for His ministry to stop. He intended for us to continue His work.

The world needs hope, and we who know the Word are just the ones to give it to them. But we will never do it **unless we get up and go.**

Look at Matthew 8:5: *And when Jesus was entered into Capernaum, there came unto him a centurion, beseeching him . . . .*

In verses 14,15 we read: *When Jesus was come into Peter's house, he saw his wife's mother laid, and sick of a fever. And he touched her hand, and the fever left her: and she arose, and ministered unto them.*

Again in verses 16,17: *. . . they brought unto him many that were possessed with devils; and he cast out the spirits with his word, and healed all that were sick: that it might be fulfilled which was spoken by Esaias the prophet, saying, Himself took our infirmities, and bare our sicknesses.*

Signs and wonders accompanied Jesus *as he went.* And not just healings. In verses 23-27 as He and His disciples were crossing the sea, a storm came up to destroy them, but Jesus rebuked the wind and the sea, *and there was a great calm* (v. 26).

Missionaries would not have all those testimonies of miracles which accompany their ministries if they had not obeyed the call, gotten up, and gone. It's the *goers* and the *doers* who have the testimonies. They are the ones having all the fun!

Jesus was always *going* and *doing.*

He *went* to a wedding feast and turned the water into wine. (John 2:1-11.) He *went* for a drink of water, met the woman at the well, and changed her life. (John 4:3-42.) He *went* to the Pool of Siloam and healed a cripple who had been sick for thirty-eight years. (John 5:1-9.)

He *multiplied* loaves and fishes on two occasions. (Matt. 14:15-21; 15:32-39). He *walked* on the water and *helped* Peter to do the same. (Matt. 14:22-33.) He *sent* Peter to catch a fish with money in its mouth to pay their taxes. (Matt. 17:27.)

His was an exciting life — one miracle after another — but it was only because He was "about His Father's business" — *going* and *saying* and *doing* what God showed Him to do.

You can do it, too. Jesus said you could. (John 14:12.)

He gave to us — to His followers — His power, His name, and His Word to accomplish His work on this earth.

We must do it!

The millions of people who haven't yet heard of God's miracle-working power deserve to.

For information regarding Burnie Davis' monthly newspaper, *Miracles Activated,* you may write:

Burnie Davis Global Ministries
P. O. Box 7148
Pasadena, TX 77505

Photographs

Burnie Davis began his ministry at 18 years of age.

Burnie Davis at a recent outdoor crusade pointing the people to Jesus.

Burnie Davis praying for the sick at an outdoor crusade. God confirmed His Word by healing the sick, and convinced the multitudes that Jesus is the only Mediator, the Way, the Truth, and the Life.

Burnie Davis preaching the Word on the Trinity Broadcasting Network in Oklahoma City.

Burnie proclaiming the Gospel to the people during a crusade.

God miraculously healed a Communist leader in a crusade in Spanish Honduras. The man accompanied his wife to the meeting because he had seen so much advertising about Jesus' power to heal. He had been to doctors in Honduras and the United States, but they were unable to find the cause or cure for his ailment which gave him great pain.

He had sent his servants to the meeting early with chairs for his family. He brought two concealed guns to the service (He was known and feared by many.) During the third night of the meetings he suddenly realized that he had no more pain. He and his entire family were born again and filled with the Holy Spirit. He immediately began to go from one businessman to another, telling them about his change and praying with them to be born again.

He has been a great witness and has helped to spread the Gospel by using his influence to open doors.

Crusade meeting in Tegusagalpa, Spanish Honduras, C.A.

The last afternoon of the crusade in San Pedro Sula, Spanish Honduras, C.A., the people made a sign: GOD BLESS YOUR CRUSADE, BROTHER BURNIE.

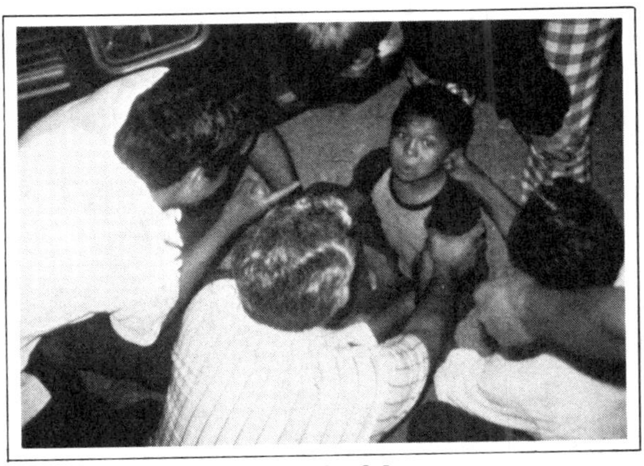

It took five men to hold this boy while they prayed and cast the demons out of him in Jesus' name. He had run away from home (40 km away) and had wandered into the crusade grounds. His family had kept him tied up and locked in a room until that night to prevent him from hurting himself. See him born again with peace and joy on his countenance and happiness on his mother's face.

A baptism after one crusade took five pastors seven hours.

Thirteen new churches were started from this crusade. When the area was visited four months later, all the churches were flourishing with attendance from 300 to 1,600 in each church.

A tent crusade in Ituverava, Brazil, a city of 35,000. An estimated 10,000 responded to the altar call during the month of services held morning and evening.

During the crusade Burnie Davis raised $300 to purchase property for a church. Later he sent $1,000 to purchase building materials.

Services continued in the tent at Ituverava, Brazil, while the church was being built.

This dying man was brought to a crusade in a taxi and carried to the platform. He was healed of stomach cancer. His swollen stomach shrank before the eyes of the crowd as God healed him.

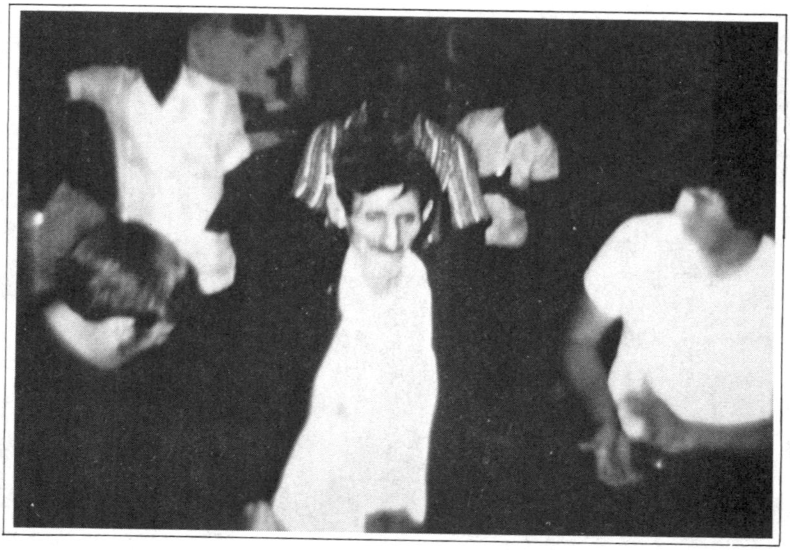

These men performed at the hotel in Trinidad, B.W.I., where Burnie and the crusade team stayed. During their performance the drummers brought the music to a fevered pitch, then the dancers' movements became frenzied. A man would then break

several bottles, setting them on fire. The dancer would walk on the broken, burning glass and then roll on it. As the beat of the drums slowed, the dancer would slow. The dancer later told Burnie that he had to have the drums at a certain beat before he could walk and roll on the burning, broken glass.

All four men were born again during the crusade.

Demon-inspired worship led by this woman in Trinidad, B.W.I.,is

very deceiving. A small amount of the Bible is preached in their street meetings to lure the people to their meeting place. This woman was called "Mother" by her followers.

Burnie Davis, preaching in Kerala, India.

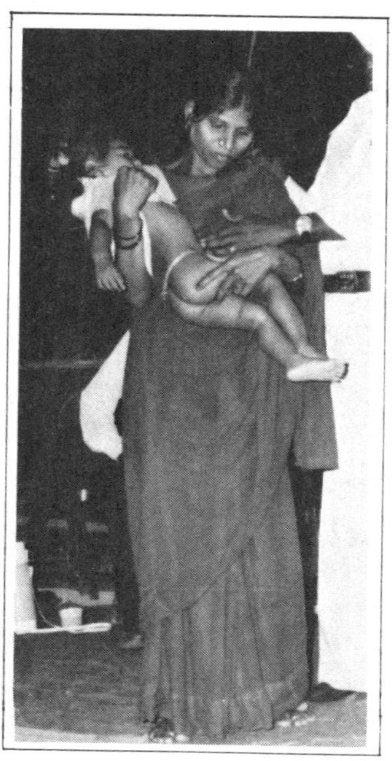

The interpreter's hand points to the place on the child's abdomen where a large tumor dissolved.

A man healed of a rupture in an India crusade.

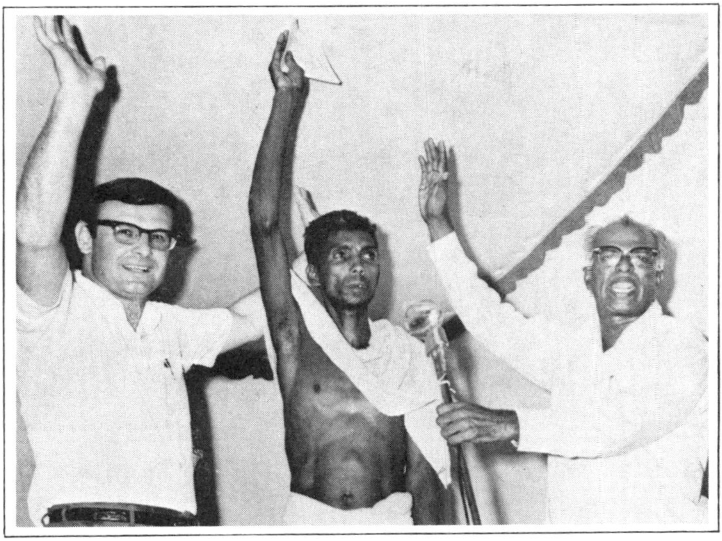

A man, both crippled and blind, received his healing while in the India crusade audience.

Thousands were saved and healed while Burnie preached the Word of God in India.

Many were healed and saved at this crusade with Evangelist K. John Sundar in Tuni, India.

These orphan children shown with Burnie in India are supported by Global Evangelism.

Burnie passing out New Testaments to the children in a public school in the Communist-ruled state of Kerala, India.

Burnie and Dolly In India.

Recently Burnie held 3 services a day. Multitudes gathered to praise the Lord.